Also by Harriet and Shirley

Glimpses of God:
a winter devotional for women

Glimpses of God:
a spring devotional for women

Glimpses of God:
a summer devotional for women

Glimpses of God:
an autumn devotional for women

Prayer Warrior Confessions

Glimpses of Prayer, a devotional

Glimpses of the Savior, a holiday devotional

By Harriet
Prayer: It's Not About You

By Shirley
Study Guide on Prayer

A Ten-week Devotional Drawn from Biblical Insights (Wonder) & Hymns of Praise (Worship)

Harriet E. Michael
Shirley Crowder

Wonder & Worship

© Copyright 2024 Harriet E. Michael & Shirley Crowder
ISBN: 978-1-951602-22-2

Published by:

 Entrusted Books, an imprint of Write Integrity Press
PO Box 702852; Dallas, TX 75370
www.WriteIntegrity.com

Published in the United States of America.

Dedication

Soli Deo Gloria!

This book is a humble offering to the glory of God
alone, who is the source
of all wisdom, truth, and beauty.

May He use it for His purposes and His kingdom.

"Not to us, Lord, not to us
but to your name be the glory,
because of your love and faithfulness."

Psalm 115:1

Wonder & Worship

Acknowledgments

Harriet especially thanks Dr. Peter Gentry, her former Sunday school teacher, Donna Pavkovich, her former Bible study teacher, and the late Mark Janke, her former preacher for their many years of wonderful teachings that she had the privilege to sit under. Many of the nuggets in this book are gleaned from their teachings.

Shirley is grateful for the many men and women who taught her Scripture and how to worship her Savior through music. In addition to her parents, the late Anne Fite Butler, her junior and senior high school voice teacher and choir leader, influenced her love for and understanding of technique in singing and playing the piano, and helped her understand the power of music.

Harriet and Shirley are thankful for their friend and publisher, Marji Laine Clubine, who has encouraged and directed them while working to bring this devotional to print and who created the cover design.

They are indebted to their missionary kid cousin, Baker Hill, who provided encouragement and guidance during the process of writing this devotional.

They appreciate fellow Write Integrity Press author, Betty Thomason Owens who helped them refine their manuscript.

Contents

Preface

"The Bible is alive, it speaks to me, it has feet, it runs after me, it has hands, it lays hold of me."
– Martin Luther

The Bible is alive, indeed. The more a person studies it, the more alive and active it becomes in their life. This devotional was written in the hopes that it will help make the Bible more alive to its readers. It is intended as not only inspirational but also educational.

Co-authors Harriet E. Michael and Shirley Crowder have written devotional books together before. This book is a little different from those and other more traditional devotionals in how it is structured. Most devotions list a suggested Scripture passage and key verse at the beginning of each daily reading, but this book will start each daily devotion a little differently.

The book is entitled "Wonder and Worship" for a reason. All the devotions fall under either the "wonder" category or the "worship" category. "Wonder" devotions are written around a lesser-known Scripture verse or biblical fact which we are calling Bible nuggets. These devotions, written by Harriet, begin with a nugget rather than a key verse. The "worship" devotions, written by Shirley, are based on a hymn that reflects the theme of the chapter or a point made in the "wonder" devotions. These will begin with a title for the

Worship Hymn Focus instead of a key verse. Writing it this way flowed naturally for Harriet and Shirley because of each of their unique talents, personalities, and experiences.

They both have engaged in many years of Bible studies. Harriet wrote the nuggets you will read because she once wrote a column for a writers' newsletter that included these and other nuggets—strange and interesting Bible facts that could be written in less than two hundred words. Harriet did this for several years and developed the habit of mining for these nuggets of wonder, just like a gold miner might mine for nuggets of gold. Such nuggets spotlight biblical points from random parts of the Bible that are lesser known, with the hope that readers who read and meditate on the devotions in this book will not just leave inspired but will also grow in their knowledge of Scripture. The hymns bring extra enhancement to these devotions. God gave Shirley an extra-large dose of musical talent. She has studied music and is an accomplished pianist who has served in that manner for several churches in her lifetime. She uses music as a means of sharing the love of Christ and encouraging others in their walk with Him.

When discussing this devotional book, the authors chose to make it similar to an organized Bible study or biblical seminar with bits of teachings interspersed with worship hymns. Imagine sitting in a conference listening to a speaker share new biblical insights that are interspersed with hymns of worship. That is what this book is like with the added perk of having these teachings and hymns of worship written in devotional form that can be read in only a few minutes.

The book is broken into two parts—interesting facts from the Old Testament and interesting facts from the New Testament. Each part has hymn-based devotions as well as devotions drawn from interesting Bible facts. The book is also organized into Bible book divisions recognized by most Bible scholars."

These are:

Old Testament:

Books of the Law—Genesis, Exodus, Leviticus, Numbers, Deuteronomy

Books of History—Joshua, Judges, Ruth, 1 & 2 Samuel, 1 & 2 Kings, 1 & 2 Chronicles, Ezra, Nehemiah, Esther

Poetry (sometimes called the Books of Wisdom)—Job, Psalms, Ecclesiastes, Song of Solomon, Lamentations

Major Propjets—Isaiah, Jeremiah, Ezekiel, Daniel

Minor Prophets—Hosea, Joel, Amos, Obadiah, Jonah, Micah, Nahum, Habakkuk, Zephaniah, Haggai, Zechariah, Malachi

New Testament

Gospels—Matthew, Mark, Luke, John

History—Acts

Pauline Epistles—Romans, 1 & 2 Corinthians, Galatians, Ephesians, Philippians, Colossians, 1 & 2

Thessalonians, 1 & 2 Timothy, Titus, Philemon
General Epistles—Hebrews, James, 1 & 2 Peter, 1, 2, &
3 John, Jude
Prophecy—Revelation

There are ten chapters, and the plan is to read one chapter a week. These will contain three devotions derived from and built around a nugget gleaned from one of the books in the chapter division, and two hymn-based devotions. Also in each week, one Fruit of the Spirit that is prominent in the devotions will be highlighted. Note that some of these divisions contain many books while others have only one book. Since the devotions in this book are divided into chapters according to these accepted biblical book categories, not all books of the Bible will have a devotion corresponding to it while at the same time some of the books will have more than one devotion that corresponds to them.

Here are three examples of Bible nuggets that contain information about the Bible in general. These particular nuggets have not been developed into devotions but will help show the type of information that each wonder devotion will contain while also educating readers on some general lesser-known facts about the Bible in general.

Nugget #1

The Bible as we know it today has chapter breaks but these were not in the original manuscripts. They were put in by Archbishop Langton who was the Archbishop of Canterbury around AD 1227. This was done to help find scriptures more easily by using both chapters and verses. When Archbishop Langton took on this task of breaking the books into chapters the verses were already there, having been numbered at least a thousand years earlier. But even verse numbering was not in the original manuscripts.

Nugget #2

The Old Testament was written in Hebrew, the New Testament in Greek. This is only a rule of thumb because some Aramaic is thrown in too (Daniel, Ezra, and a few other places). I had many years of Bible study before I knew this. But once explained it made so much sense! Given to the Jews, the Old Testament was written in their language. But just prior to Christ's birth, Alexander the Great conquered the known world, making Greek the common language, so the writers of the New Testament used Greek.

Nugget #3

Hebrews 12:29 says, "For our God is a consuming fire." And Isaiah 33:14 asks the question, "Who can live with a consuming fire?" Moses, however, saw a bush that was on fire but not consumed and in Exodus when God led His people as a pillar of fire at night it was again a fire that did not consume. What are we to think then? What is the answer to the question posed in Isaiah? Here's the answer—no one can live with a consuming fire which God indeed is to sinners who die without Christ. But to believers God is a fire that does not consume.

...and so our journey begins as we look closer at this consuming fire that does not consume those who believe in Him.

The Fruit of the Spirit

This book is divided into ten chapters. Our first chapter focuses on holiness, the foundation upon which the other chapters are built. God's holiness, the God-ness of God, means that He is separate from everything that is not God. He is absolutely holy—in a class all by Himself.

The subsequent nine chapters will focus on one of the Fruit of the Spirit: love, joy, peace, patience, kindness, goodness, faithfulness, gentleness, and self-control.

In Galatians 5:19-21, the Apostle Paul tells us to "walk by the Spirit" so we will not "gratify the desires of the flesh." Paul then contrasts these desires of the flesh with the godly fruit of the Spirit, "But the fruit of the Spirit is love, joy, peace, patience, kindness, goodness, faithfulness, gentleness, and self-control" (Galatians 5:22-23 ESV).

Paul uses the singular, fruit, here. He refers to a bundle of qualities. This fruit is not like a menu where we pick and choose ones we want. The evidence of a person's relationship with Christ—that the Holy Spirit resides in their life—is the presence and manifestation of the fruit of the Spirit. Each Christ-follower is responsible for choosing to exercise each of the fruit in their life. This choosing requires us to confess our sin, turn away from the desires of the flesh, and choose to exhibit the fruit.

It is only through the power and guidance of the Holy

Spirit that we are able to manifest the fruit of the Spirit. As we grow in our relationship with God through spending time reading, studying, memorizing, contemplating, and meditating upon His Word, we are transformed more and more into His image. Our response to the indwelling Holy Spirit's work is choosing to develop and exhibit the fruit of His Spirit in and through us.

Let's prepare our hearts to receive God's encouragement to "walk by the Spirit" as we exhibit and exercise the fruit of the Spirit.

Old Testament

The Old Testament makes three main points: there is only one true God, that God is in a covenant relationship with His people, and when His people get into trouble, He is bound by that covenant to get involved in their lives and help them. – Septuagint scholar, Dr. Peter Gentry

The greatest example of this is seen in the New Testament when God got involved in the lives of His sin-troubled people and sent His Son to save them. – Harriet E. Michael

Week One

Holiness

Nuggets of Wonder from the Books of the Law

The first five books of the Old Testament are called "The Law." In Judaism, they're called The Torah, which means law, or The Pentateuch, which means five scrolls.

Although they teach God's law, they also include history from creation to the arrival of the Israelites in the Promised Land. God gave Moses most of the Law when the Israelites were camped around Mt. Sinai. The Law served two purposes. It showed the world that people who follow Him act differently than people who don't, and it reinforced the truth that no one can ever be good enough to earn God's love.[1]

The five books of the Law are: Genesis, Exodus, Leviticus, Numbers, Deuteronomy.

Foundation for the Fruit of the Spirit—Holiness

Before we look at the Fruit of the Spirit, let's look at the holiness of God—the fertile soil in which the fruit of the Spirit flourishes.

Holy means to be set apart, cut off from, or separated. God's holiness is unsurpassed. God is separate from

---

[1] What is the Story of The Law Books in the Old Testament? (compellingtruth.org) accessed 8/3/22

everything that is not God—He is in a class by Himself. Holiness starts with God. R. C. Sproul said the holiness of God "...is basic to our whole understanding of God and of Christianity."[2]

First Peter 1:16 tells us to "be holy because I am holy." When we speak of our being holy, we mean that we are separated from the secular and devoted to God. We can be holy because Holy God, through His Son Jesus, pardons our sin and enables us to be holy. As we seek holiness, we seek the Holy One who counted us holy and continues making us holy through the process of sanctification.

"Consecrate yourselves and be holy, because I am the LORD your God. Keep my decrees and follow them. I am the LORD, who makes you holy" (Leviticus 20:7).

---

[2] Sproul, R. C. (2009). *The Holiness of God*. Tyndale House Publishers. https://www.amazon.com/KindleEditions/B00ZRPX97C, page 12, location 326.

Day One: A Holy God

By Harriet

Today's Bible Nugget

When Jacob left the Promised Land, he encountered angels (Genesis 28:12-17). When he returned to the Promised Land, he again encountered angels (Genesis 32:24 -29). My late pastor, Mark Janke, once said in a sermon that Dr. Sailhamer, one of his graduate school professors, connected these passages to the Garden of Eden where God posted angels at the gate after forcing Adam and Eve to leave (Genesis 3). Pastor Mark said the Old Testament Promised Land is like the Garden of Eden and they are both shadows of which the New Heaven and New Earth will be the realities.

Holiness.

We've all heard the term, but we often don't fully understand its meaning. When I looked it up in an online dictionary, they defined holiness as the state of being holy. Well… that's not much help if you don't know what holy means. As a teenager, I heard the word holy used in slang as an exclamation of surprise. I grew up at a time when people sometimes exclaimed, "Holy smoke" when taken by surprise as in, "Holy smoke! That car nearly hit me." The use of the word holy as slang was largely due to the Batman TV series that ran from 1966 to 1968. In that series Batman's sidekick,

Robin, usually exclaimed "holy something" at least once per episode and often several times. In one of season two's episodes entitled, "Hot off the Griddle," he exclaimed, "Holy oleo!" referring to a margarine that was popular at the time.

The subsequent verbal exchange had Catwoman retorting, "I didn't know you could yodel."

Of course, this use of holy has nothing to do with the real meaning of the words holy and holiness, especially as they are used in the Bible. Instead, this slang popularized in the 1960s only added to the general confusion over what it really means to be holy. And while we're asking questions, what does holiness have to do with angels?

Angels are seen in Scripture declaring God's holiness in a few places. The prophet Isaiah gives us a glimpse of God's throne room through a vision he had. In this vision, found in Isaiah 6:2-3, we see a special type of angel called seraphim. They fly around God's throne and call to each other saying, "Holy, holy, holy is the Lord Almighty, the whole earth is full of his glory." This scene occurs again in the apostle John's vision in Revelation 4:8.

Angels are described in Scripture in ways that strike awe in me. The angel mentioned in today's nugget that was placed at the gate of the Garden of Eden held a fiery sword in his hand. In another of Isaiah's visions, an angel is seen carrying a burning coal to Isaiah that the angel then touched to Isaiah's lips to cleanse them after Isaiah said they were unclean. In Genesis 32:25, an angel knocks Jacob's hip out of joint with just one touch, and in 2 Kings 6:17 angels show up as an army with horses and chariots of fire. All of these mental images—angels holding fiery swords and able to touch hot coals without being burned, an angel with enough strength in his finger to knock a man's hip out of joint with just a touch, armies of angels in fiery chariots, and strangely described angelic beings flying around God's throne declaring His holiness—all worked together to forge an image in my heart and mind as a child that whatever holy was, and whatever it meant to be holy, it was pretty important and largely beyond my ability to achieve.

These mental images, which were too grand for my little-girl mind, had me believing that to be holy must require a level of perfection that I knew I could never master. Instead of encouraging me to strive to be holy, I found myself discouraged because like Isaiah, I too was an unclean person living among other unclean people in an unclean world. I held on to this concept well into my adult years. Maybe that's where you are too. You may find yourself reading this and thinking, like I did, that personal holiness is something you desire in your life—after all, it's what the Bible calls us to be in 1 Peter 1:15-16 where it says, "But just as he who called you is holy, so be holy in all you do; for it is written: 'Be holy, because I am holy.'" Yet, it seems impossible to ever reach a state of holiness. Hang in there. What it really means to be holy will be better explained in Day Three of this week's devotions and you will see that it is not an impossible mountain to climb.

Prayer: Heavenly Father, You are holy, and You call us to be holy too. But we are sinful, unclean people. Touch our lives with Your holiness and teach us how to be holy too. In Jesus' name, Amen.

Thought for the Day: God takes holiness seriously.

Day Two: Holy, Holy, Holy

By Shirley

Worship Hymn Focus
Holy, Holy, Holy
1826 by Reginald Heber

God's holiness is the fertile soil in which the fruit of the Spirit grows. Through our understanding of God's holiness, we gain a fuller understanding of how to cultivate and exhibit holiness in our own lives.

As we read in the previous devotional, Isaiah saw a glorious and reassuring sight—the Sovereign God of the Universe sitting on His throne. It is as if Isaiah pulled aside a curtain and gave us a glimpse into God's throne room.

The seraphim were flying above the throne (Isaiah 6). God's presence produced a profound sense of awe, reverence, and respect in the seraphim who responded in humble submission to, and respect for, Holy God.

The seraphim model for us how to respond to the holiness of God. They call out to each other, "Holy, holy, holy is the LORD Almighty; the whole earth is full of his glory" (Isaiah 6:3). God is always on His throne! He was, is, and evermore shall be the living God.

We see that we are to approach God with an intense reverence while acknowledging our unworthiness to behold His glory. We approach God fully aware of our sin. We should always be ready and quick to praise and serve God.

Isaiah's vision destroys our incorrect view of how we are to approach God and reminds us that God is so holy and magnificent that we cannot approach Him except through the shed blood of Jesus.

Reginald Heber wrote the words of the majestic hymn, "Holy, Holy, Holy!" that echoes the Isaiah 6 passage and then describes aspects of God's character for which we praise Him.

Stanza 1
Holy, holy, holy! Lord God Almighty!
Early in the morning our song shall rise to Thee;
Holy, holy, holy, merciful and mighty!
God in three Persons, blessed Trinity!

God directed Moses to tell the Israelites, "I the LORD your God, am holy" (Leviticus 19:2). In recognition of His holiness, mercy, and might, we sing praises to the Triune God (Matthew 28:19).

Stanza 2
Holy, holy, holy! All the saints adore Thee,
Casting down their golden crowns around the glassy sea;
Cherubim and seraphim falling down before Thee,
Who was, and is, and evermore shall be.

Following the seraphim's model of how we are to interact with Holy God, every saint—redeemed person—will cast (lay) his crown before the throne of God. Since God is the One who gives the crowns, the saints offer those crowns back to Him, acknowledging that He alone is worthy of our praise (Revelation 4:9-11). While singing this stanza, picture the seraphim from Isaiah 6 worshiping God.

We worship and adore God because He is "'the Lord God Almighty,' who was, and is, and is to come" (Revelation 4:8).

Stanza 3
Holy, holy, holy! Though the darkness hide Thee,
Though the eye of sinful man Thy glory may not see;
Only Thou art holy; there is none beside Thee,
Perfect in pow'r, in love, and purity.

This stanza focuses on God's perfection. Our sin—the darkness—keeps us from seeing God clearly. I am reminded of Exodus 33:18-23 when Moses asked God to show him His glory. We, like Moses, could not bear to see the full glory of God—His holiness, perfection, majesty, and might. No one else is holy like God whose power, love, and purity are perfect—that is why we praise Him (Exodus 15:11).

Stanza 4
Holy, holy, holy! Lord God Almighty!
All Thy works shall praise Thy Name,
in earth, and sky, and sea;
Holy, holy, holy; merciful and mighty!
God in three Persons, blessed Trinity!

We praise Almighty God for His omnipotence which we see in everything that He created (Romans 1:20). All of creation praises Him. For example, "Let all creation rejoice before the LORD" (Psalm 96:13). This stanza ends with the same two lines as we ended the first stanza, recognizing God's holiness, mercy, and might, as we sing praises to the Triune God (2 Corinthians 13:14).

Prayer: Holy God, forgive us for the casual and often lazy way we approach You. Thank You for making a way for us—sinful as we are—to approach You and have a personal relationship with You through the shed blood of Your Son, Jesus, in whose name we pray, Amen.

Thought for the Day: "May he strengthen your hearts so that you will be blameless and holy in the presence of our God and Father when our Lord Jesus comes with all his holy ones" (1 Thessalonians 3:13).

Day Three: What It Means To Be Holy

By Harriet

Today's Bible Nugget

In Exodus 3:5 God tells Moses to take off his sandals because he is standing on holy ground. What is meant by the term "holy" in the context of God's instruction to remove the sandals? The Hebrews removed a sandal when they gave up rights to something. An example of this is seen in Ruth 4:8. Ruth's next of kin took off his sandal as he gave up his rights to Ruth, allowing Boaz to have her. So, when God told Moses to take off his sandals, Moses was giving up the rights to that piece of land. It now belonged to God. If we are a holy people, we are a consecrated people; a people owned by God, not ourselves.

When I was twenty years old, a young man I was dating and had fallen in love with, popped the question to me, asking me to marry him. He had come with my family and me on a visit to my uncle's farm. We had some free time before supper, so we walked around the farm. We stopped at the barn and climbed up into the hayloft to get a better view of the creek and pasture. There sitting next to me he said, "You will marry me, won't you?"

"Is that a proposal?" I asked.

This was a bit of a joke between us because a few weeks

earlier he had commented on how much he was paying in long-distance phone calls to me during the weeks while I was away at college. I came home on weekends and sometimes in the middle of the week to see him, but we were apart during many of the weekdays. He had said it would be cheaper to buy me a ring than to make all those calls. Immediately, he realized how that sounded and responded with a jolt as if struck by lightning, exclaiming, "That was not a proposal." At the time, I just laughed and saluted in a "Yes, sir," gesture which made us both laugh.

So, when he said what he did in my uncle's hayloft, I knew he was asking me to marry him but teased back asking if it was actually a proposal this time. He said it was and I replied, "Yes, I will marry you."

It was that simple. Just like that, we were engaged. We were adults who could make decisions for ourselves, because in the American culture where we lived, those were the rules. They were the cultural norms. I loved him, he loved me, and our culture said the decision to marry was up to us. It's a decision we are both still glad we made forty-plus years, four children, and five grandchildren later.

Back in the days of Ruth and Boaz, this freedom to choose a spouse did not exist. The ancient Hebrews had strict rules about who could marry whom. According to these Jewish laws, Boaz was second in line to marry Ruth. In order to have her, the man who was first in line had to give up his rights to her. This is exactly what happened. And what did this man do to symbolize he was giving up his rights to Ruth? He took off his sandal and gave it to Boaz. Ruth 4:7 states it clearly when it says, "...for the redemption of property to become final, one party took off his sandal and gave it to the other. This was the method of legalizing transactions..."

I've heard this story all my life and never connected it to Moses and the burning bush until one day in Sunday school, when my teacher, Dr. Peter Gentry, drew the connection for me. Today's nugget is drawn from what he said that day. Dr. Gentry first asked us what we thought holy meant. Several class members offered answers like sinless, perfect, pure, undefiled. Then Dr. Gentry read the passage where God tells Moses he is standing on holy ground and asked us if that ground could be sinless, perfect, pure, or undefiled? Then he reminded us of the story of Boaz and Ruth and explained that removing a sandal was the way a person in those days showed they were giving up their rights to something. When God said the ground Moses stood on was holy, He did not mean it was perfect or sinless, or undefiled. God meant it belonged to Him and He was setting it apart for His purposes. That piece of land no longer belonged to Moses—it belonged to God. In taking off his sandal, Moses was giving up his right to the land.

So, what are we to conclude it means to be holy? By looking at the Scripture that my Sunday school teacher connected for my class that Sunday morning a few years ago, it would seem being holy means our lives no longer belong to us. Instead, we belong to God and are set apart for His purposes. Somehow this feels less overwhelming and more achievable to me. I can live in a holy manner not because I can live a life that is perfect or even sinless, but rather, I can live a life that is not my own. I belong to God and am set apart by Him for His purposes.

Prayer: Father, You have bought me with a price. I belong to You. Help me to live in a way that is honoring to You. In Jesus' name, Amen.

Thought for the Day: My life is not my own. I am God's and am set apart for His purposes.

Day Four: Take Time to Be Holy

By Shirley

Worship Hymn Focus
Take Time to Be Holy
1882 by William D. Longstaff

God "chose us in him before the creation of the world to be holy and blameless in his sight" (Ephesians 1:4).

Perhaps hearing this is daunting to you. We have looked at God's holiness and what it means to be holy (set apart for God). Isn't it great to know that if God has set us apart for something that He will enable us to be or do that thing?

When we are saved, the Holy Spirit indwells us. It is through His enablement that we can be holy. We don't immediately become holy. Developing holiness requires our taking time and making the effort to know God's Word so that we know God and what He requires of us. We must engage in prayer, be diligent to confess and repent of sin when the Holy Spirit convicts us, and be sensitive to His leading and enabling power to live a holy life.

William D. Longstaff wrote the lyrics for the instructive hymn "Take Time to Be Holy" that reminds us that we are holy because God is holy (Leviticus 19:2b).

Stanza 1
Take time to be holy, speak oft with thy Lord;
Abide in Him always, and feed on His Word.

Make friends of God's children, help those who are weak,
Forgetting in nothing His blessing to seek.

We can be holy by praying often. We are to remain in the Lord by delighting in and meditating on His Word (Psalm 1:2). Other Christ-followers help us protect our walk with Christ. As we pray, read God's Word, and spend time with other Christ-followers, we are to help those around us who are in need. We are to glorify God in and through everything we think, say, and do.

Stanza 2
Take time to be holy, the world rushes on;
Spend much time in secret, with Jesus alone.
By looking to Jesus, like Him thou shalt be;
Thy friends in thy conduct His likeness shall see.

In the midst of the busyness—often chaos—of our lives, time alone with Christ in prayer and Bible study is very important. As we look to, and learn about, Jesus through the Bible, we will live according to His commands and become more like Him (1 John 2:6). If we are truly seeking to be holy, we will let our "light shine before others, that they may see your good deeds and glorify your Father in heaven" (Matthew 5:16).

Stanza 3
Take time to be holy, let Him be thy Guide;
And run not before Him, whatever betide.

In joy or in sorrow, still follow the Lord,
And, looking to Jesus, still trust in His Word.

Part of being holy is trusting God's leading, following Him, and not running ahead of Him, even when His timing is not ours, and His leading takes us where we do not want to go. At such times, remember Jesus' command to "deny [our] selves and take up [our] cross and follow [Him]" (Matthew 16:24). We are to "trust in the Lord with all [our] heart and lean not on [our] own understanding" (Proverbs 3:5).

Stanza 4
Take time to be holy, be calm in thy soul,
Each thought and each motive beneath His control.
Thus led by His Spirit to fountains of love,
Thou soon shalt be fitted for service above.

Holiness enables us to trust God more fully; thus, we are calm. We are led by the Holy Spirit through the Bible as He prompts, teaches, and guides us (Romans 8:14), so we "live in accordance with the Spirit and have [our] minds set on what the Spirit desires" (Romans 8:5b). By taking "captive every thought to make it obedient to Christ" (2 Corinthians 10:5), we "make every effort to add to [our] faith goodness; and to goodness, knowledge; and to knowledge, self-control; and to self-control, perseverance; and to perseverance, godliness; and to godliness, mutual affection; and to mutual affection, love. For if you possess these qualities in increasing measure, they will keep [us] from being ineffective and unproductive in [our] knowledge of our Lord Jesus Christ" (2 Peter 1:5-8).

Prayer: Heavenly Father, thank You for Your Holy Spirit who teaches, enables, leads, and empowers us to be holy. Help us focus our time and attention on praying and spending time with You. In Jesus' name, Amen.

Thought for the Day: Take time to be holy!

Day Five: The Splendor of His Holiness

By Harriet

Today's Bible Nugget

When Adam and Eve were forced to leave the Garden of Eden, they could no longer see God's face. Moses was not allowed to see God's face either, but in Revelation man finally sees God's face. It takes the entire Bible to show us how man gets to this blessed place of finally seeing God's face. 1 Corinthians 13:12 assures us of this, "For now we see in a mirror dimly, but then face to face, now I know in part but then I shall know fully just as I am fully known" (NASB).

In day three of this week, we saw that being holy means we belong to God. When will we belong to God more fully than the day we leave our earthly bodies and find ourselves in heaven in the actual presence of God?

My mother passed away unexpectedly in August of 2019. On a Wednesday evening, she walked into her new church building to view the classroom where she would be teaching Sunday school the following Sunday. At eighty-six, Mom had taught Sunday school for many years and with the completion of her church's new building, her class would be meeting in a brand-new room in just a few days. That Wednesday evening, Mom looked over her new room and decided there weren't enough chairs, so she put in a request for more chairs. She was a popular teacher and her previous room had been overflowing with women who loved her teaching. But apart from the need for more chairs, she loved her new classroom. Little did she know she would never teach a lesson in it. The next day her small intestine twisted inside her, requiring one surgery and then another. On the following Sunday, instead of teaching in her new classroom, she lay sedated in a hospital bed in the ICU, and on Monday she died.

A few days before all this happened, I dreamed about my mom. It was a simple dream. Mom and Dad stood near a concrete wall that was only about four feet high. Well, Daddy stood. Mom sat on the wall with her legs crossed at the knees, smiling. There was water behind them and sloping concrete in front of the partial wall. It looked as if they were on a boat dock. My parents served as missionaries in Nigeria and their first trip out, they rode an ocean liner. I've seen pictures of them boarding that boat and this scene in my dream is reminiscent of that picture. So, I immediately thought they were waiting to board a boat and travel somewhere.

The unusual thing about my dream was that my father appeared his age—ninety at the time—but Mom looked young, healthy, radiant, and oh, so beautiful! She had a radiance and serenity about her like nothing I'd ever seen before. My mother was a pretty woman but, in my dream, not only did she not look eighty-six, she had a beauty that exceeded any I'd ever seen.

I remembered my dream the next morning on my drive

to work, and as I did, I felt a deep unexplainable ache in my heart like I was missing her and yearning for her. We didn't live close, so there were times I missed her, but this felt different. I ached for her as though I would never see her again. In my car that morning I shook it off, thinking how silly I was to miss her so much when I could pick up my phone and call her anytime I wanted. I resolved to call her that night but then I talked myself into waiting until the weekend, since weekdays are so full of activity. I never got to call her. By the weekend, she was heavily sedated and by Monday she'd stepped into eternity.

It's not my intention in this devotion to get into dreams in general and what they might or might not mean. All I know is that this dream stuck with me. Even now I can see my mom looking younger, healthier, happier, and more beautiful than I'd ever seen her. It's interesting to me that in the dream, my parents were getting ready to go on a journey, but Daddy still looked like his old self. His body had not been transformed. Mom, on the other hand, was changed. And then in just a few days' time, she was indeed changed, transformed, and making that journey. And though my dad will likely make that journey before I do, he is still alive as I am writing this, having lived a few years now as a widower.

Today when I think back on it all, it feels like God let me have a glimpse of what my mom will look like when I see her again in heaven. Psalm 96:9 says, "Worship the LORD in the splendor of his holiness…" That's what I think I saw in my dream—Mom enjoying the splendor of God's holiness. Heaven is a mystery to us. No one living really knows what it will be like, but we do know it will be a place where the perishable will be exchanged for the unperishable. We—our bodies that can get old and disease-ridden, our minds that can lack understanding, and our hearts that can fail God and fall into sin even when we know better—will all be changed, transformed. We will fully belong to God and be completely set aside for His purposes, unencumbered by things of this world. We will be truly holy and spend all eternity enjoying the splendor of God's holiness.

Prayer: Oh Father, what an awesome reality lies ahead for we who are believers in Jesus. We hold on in faith now to what we will someday see when our faith becomes sight, and we are truly holy. In Jesus' name, Amen.

Thought for the Day: There is nothing more wonderful than being claimed by God and set apart for His purposes… being a part of the splendor of His holiness.

Week Two:

Patience

Nuggets of Wonder from the Books of Old Testament History

The next twelve books in the Old Testament are known as the books of History because they record the history of the children of Israel from when they reached the Promised Land, up to their exile into foreign kingdoms. This covers the period from when there were judges over Israel, to when it was one kingdom under kings Saul, David, and Solomon, and also through the period when the kingdom of Israel split into two kingdoms—Judah, also called the southern kingdom, and Israel, also called the northern kingdom. The final history recorded in these books is the period when both were exiled, with the northern kingdom being taken into exile by the Assyrians and the southern kingdom by the Babylonians.

The Books of History are: Joshua, Judges, Ruth, 1 & 2 Samuel, 1 & 2 Kings, 1 & 2 Chronicles, Ezra, Nehemiah, and Esther.

Fruit of the Spirit, Patience

This week the focus is on the fruit of the Spirit, patience. The Greek word *makrothumia* which means longsuffering and patience is translated in different versions of the Bible as longsuffering, perseverance, and endurance. The idea is that the Holy Spirit enables us to wait on the Lord without losing hope, letting anger control us, or admitting defeat.

"James, a servant of God and of the Lord Jesus Christ, To the twelve tribes scattered among the nations: Greetings. Consider it pure joy, my brothers and sisters, whenever you face trials of many kinds, because you know that the testing of your faith produces perseverance. Let perseverance finish its work so that you may be mature and complete, not lacking anything" (James 1:1-4).

Day One: Learning to be Patient

By Harriet

Today's Bible Nugget

In the Bible a scribe was a writer. The best-known scribe was Ezra, who penned four Old Testament books: 1 & 2 Chronicles, Ezra, and Nehemiah. Ezra 7:6 tells us that Ezra was no ordinary scribe. He was skilled in the ways of the Lord. Just like Ezra differed from other scribes, as Christian writers we are different from other writers because, also like Ezra, we know the ways of the Lord. Jesus said this about God-fearing writers: "Every scribe who has become a disciple of the kingdom of heaven is like a head of a household, who brings forth out of his treasure things new and old" (Matthew 13:52).

"Patience is a virtue."

My mother told me this many times when I was growing up. Patience didn't come easy for me. It seems God knew I needed to learn it, so He has given me many opportunities in life to learn and grow in my patience. These "opportunities" were dressed up as difficult long periods of waiting for one thing or another.

As a child, I was forced to learn patience as I waited for our goods to arrive in barrels weeks and sometimes months after my family had gotten to our destination, whether that was Africa or back to America. These barrels had all my toys in them. What a happy day when they finally arrived.

The more experiences we have that require waiting, the more patience we gain. Patience is one of the fruit of the Spirit listed in Galatians 5:22-23. Just prior to this passage, Paul mentions "the acts of the flesh." These are recognizably terrible sinful activities such as sexual immorality, impurity, hatred, discord, and selfish ambition, just to name a few. Paul contrasts these acts with "the fruit of the Spirit." Often a direct connection can be made between one of the acts of the flesh and a fruit of the Spirit, where the lack of a particular fruit of the Spirit can be seen as the root cause of one of the acts of the flesh. This is the case for patience and several of the others also. Sexual immorality, for instance, happens when a person acts on a desire rather than waiting patiently for God to fulfill that desire in His timing. Likewise, selfish gain often results from a person's inability to wait and attain his or her goal through the normal channels, which usually involve hard work.

Our Bible nugget today talks about Ezra, the scribe. Oh, the patience it must have taken to be a writer back in Ezra's day. The nuggets in this book were originally written by me for a Christian newsletter that one of my writer-friends sent out. That explains why this one and a few others seem to apply specifically to writers. A career in writing, whether Christian or secular, is a job that involves a lot of waiting. My first book took four years to write and then another seven years before I landed a book contract with a traditional publisher. A few times I've written articles as the inspiration hit me but then they sat, and some still sit, on my computer, unpublished for years. One such article was a short memoir I wrote about my high school's Cinderella run to capture the AAA state football championship. That article sat on my computer unpublished for years, gaining only a growing collection of rejection slips from magazines to which I submitted it. Finally, about five years after I wrote it, a large regional magazine picked it up and ran it in a beautiful two-page spread that included pictures from that team—of me as a cheerleader and of the team holding the championship trophy. My patience paid off as the satisfaction of seeing it in print was made even sweeter from having to wait.

It's ironic that as a little girl who had so much trouble waiting patiently for my toys to arrive, I grew up to work in a profession where forward progress is often at a snail's pace. Famous author George Orwell wrote in his 1947 essay *Why I Write,* "Writing a book is a horrible, exhausting struggle, like a long bout of some painful illness."

Today I have the benefit of writing with the use of a computer where I can cut and paste words, autosave my work, set my format for an entire piece in one action, or delete any changes I wish to make without having to completely rewrite everything for the sake of the change. Back in Orwell's day, he at least had a typewriter with a way to get rid of the letters or words and type over them fairly easily using a white typing strip or a product he could buy for that purpose. Back in Ezra's time he and other scribes had to write everything by hand on parchment or papyrus. I don't fully understand how they did this, but I know it was tedious and took a lot of patience.

How is God growing patience in your life? Maybe you are waiting for God to bring you a spouse. Perhaps you are frustrated at not being able to conceive a child, or maybe you have children and can't wait until they grow up. Perhaps it's a promotion or forward movement in your career you are wishing would happen sooner rather than later. Whatever it is, your period of waiting will grow and stretch you in ways that will increase your patience and, like my mother used to tell me, that is a virtue.

Prayer: Father, learning patience is not easy and sometimes even painful. Yet, it is something You desire us to learn and is one of the proofs that we have Your Spirit in us. Teach us patience and open our eyes to see that the long, trying seasons of waiting are blessings from You. In Jesus' name, Amen.

Thought for the Day: Patience is a virtue indeed, but it's sometimes hard to achieve.

Day Two: O Patient, Spotless One![3]

By Shirley

Worship Hymn Focus
O Patient, Spotless One
1869 by Christian Andreas Bernstein

As God is patient with us, we gain a fuller understanding of how to cultivate and exhibit the fruit of patience in our own lives.

Most of the time when I hear people speak about the characteristics of God, I hear about His mercy, grace, and love. Rarely do I hear people speak of the patience of God. Oh, how grateful I am for God's patience.

I often see the first part of Nahum 1:3 quoted on social media, "The LORD is slow to anger." This is a glorious truth about Him. Some people think that the patience or longsuffering of God show His weakness. They have not read the next part of this verse which says He is "great in power." God's patience is one of the ways He displays His power.

As we take a closer look at this entire verse, we understand God's patience more fully.

"The LORD is slow to anger but great in power; the LORD will not leave the guilty unpunished. His way is in the whirlwind and the storm, and clouds are the dust of his feet" (Nahum 1:3).

---

[3] O patient, spotless One! | Hymnary.org

God is omnipotent and all-powerful. We can trust Him to help because we know He has the power to do so. In 1 Timothy 1:16 God's mercy and love are displayed through His patience. "But for that very reason I was shown mercy so that in me, the worst of sinners, Christ Jesus might display His immense patience as an example for those who would believe in Him and receive eternal life."

Yet, He will also judge us. We do not really like talking about the judgment of God but be assured that God will judge in, and with, power. In that judgment, every sin committed by every person will be paid for either by the shed blood of Jesus Christ on the cross or by spending an eternity in hell separated from God.

Christian Andreas Bernstein wrote the engaging hymn, "O Patient, Spotless One!" that helps us understand the patience of God.

Stanza 1
O Patient, spotless One!
Our hearts in meekness train,
To bear Thy yoke, and learn of Thee,
That we may rest obtain.

We begin by calling on God who is patient with us. He is spotless, perfect, and just (Deuteronomy 32:4). He wants us to humbly submit to His training, through His Word, so that our hearts are trained (Psalm 86:11). When we "meditate on [His] precepts and consider [His] ways" (Psalm 119:15), we have "the promise of entering his rest" (Hebrews 4:1) by casting all our fears, doubts, anxieties, and cares upon Him.

Stanza 2
Jesus, Thou art enough
The mind and heart to fill;
Thy life, to calm the anxious soul,
Thy love, its fear dispel.

Second Peter 1:2-3 reminds us that God is enough to fill our minds and hearts. "Grace and peace [are ours] in abundance through the knowledge of God and of Jesus our Lord. His divine power has given us everything we need for a godly life through our knowledge of him who called us by his own glory and goodness." Our minds and hearts are transformed by the continual renewing of our minds (Romans 12:2). As we trust in God, He will calm our anxious souls and dispel our fears.

Stanza 3
O fix our earnest gaze
So wholly, Lord, on Thee,
That, with Thy beauty occupied,
We elsewhere none may see.

When we pray, let's ask God to help us fix "our eyes on Jesus, the pioneer and perfector of faith" (Hebrews 12:2). The Psalmist tells us how to walk in step with God. We are to delight and meditate upon the law of the Lord, day and night.

This means that we must focus our attention on Jesus Christ and His Word. By fixing our eyes on Him, we are able to "throw off everything that hinders and the sin that so easily entangles. And let us run with perseverance the race marked out for us" (Hebrews 12:1). We are able to have this unhindered focus on the Lord because we are captivated by the display of His beauty.

Because of the patience of God, we are able to train our minds and hearts, obtain rest, and be patient. We can fix our eyes on Him and honor Him in what we say, think, and do.

Prayer: Heavenly Father, thank You for Your patience that manifests itself through Your love, mercy, and grace. Teach us to be patient with others. In Jesus' name, Amen.

Thought for the Day: Jesus is enough to fill our hearts and minds.

Day Three: Are We There Yet?

By Harriet

Today's Bible Nugget

When God led the Israelites out of Egypt, He went before them in a cloud by day and a pillar of fire by night. (Exodus 13:22) How was this evidence of God's provision as well as His presence? They traveled through the desert. Have you ever spent time in a desert? It's hot during the day and cold at night. The temperature differences can sometimes be extreme. What did God do? He displayed His presence in the form of a cloud during the day which must have helped to block the blazing desert sun and in the form of fire at night providing a source of heat during the cold nights.

In 1752, Benjamin Franklin tied a metal key to the string of a kite and walked out into a field during a thunderstorm hoping to prove his theory that the electricity in lightning could be channeled into a metal object. His experiment resulted in the discovery of what we have come to know as electricity. Today electricity is channeled into many different uses, but it wasn't until after World War I that electricity became prevalent throughout most of the western world. That's a period of 175 years. Even today, well over 250 years later, there are still places in the world that have no electricity.

In 1172, a few stones were laid on a plot of land and

became the base of the building that we now know as the Leaning Tower of Pisa. The construction on this building continued for the next 199 years before it was finally completed. The building was not intended to lean. That occurred during the many years of construction because the soft ground could not properly support it. Today it has been reinforced so it is stable in spite of the lean.

When God led the children of Israel out of Egypt to the Promised Land, an event that is referenced in today's nugget, God allowed them to wander in the wilderness for forty years before finally arriving at their destination.

What do these have in common? They all took a lot longer than one might think they would or should. If electricity was as much of an amazing discovery as it turned out to be, why did it take so long to become widely used? If God intended the children of Israel to one day arrive at the land He had promised them, why did He have them wandering in the wilderness for so long? Perhaps it's better to ask what the people learned during these long periods of waiting than to ask why it took so long.

In the case of the electricity and the Tower of Pisa, certainly people learned many things about science and architecture. In the case of the children of Israel wandering in the wilderness, what they learned was of a spiritual nature. They learned to trust in God's leadership and to trust Him for their protection and provision; they learned that He keeps His promises, but they also learned that His timing was not their timing. They learned patience.

Patience is defined as "The capacity to accept or tolerate delay or suffering without getting angry or upset." In my life, I've found the accepting and tolerating part to be a little easier to do than the suffering part. Can waiting really cause suffering? Can it be painful to wait for something? The answer, of course, is yes. It really can be painful both emotionally and physically, depending on what a person might be waiting for. Shirley has a nephew who suffered a severe burn in a major condo fire. Today his body is healed, and he is no longer in pain, but waiting for that healing to occur during repeated dressing changes and skin graft surgeries was not just painful, it was excruciatingly painful.

When riding in a car on a long family trip, children often ask, "Are we there yet?" I and my siblings used to ask that question of our parents, and my children used to ask it of my husband and me. Can you imagine how many times the children of Israel must have said this to poor Moses during those long forty years of wilderness wandering? But, oh, the patience they must have gained.

Prayer: Heavenly Father, Your timing is perfect but sometimes that perfect timing requires us to live through what feels like a long period of waiting that can be agonizing to us. Help us to hold on to faith and to rest in the truth that Your timing is perfect indeed. In Jesus' name, Amen.

Thought for the Day: What is God requiring you to wait on? Rest assured, He has not forgotten you or your situation.

Day Four: Wait, and Murmur Not[4]

By Shirley

Worship Hymn Focus
Wait, and Murmur Not
1879 by William Henry Bellamy

Patience—the fruit of the Spirit we want everyone to have toward us, but we are not nearly as eager to offer to others. Yet, God is patient with us, and He also grants patience to us freely as one of the fruit of His Spirit. Surely, we can work more diligently at showing this fruit in our lives as we interact with others.

The Apostle Paul gave us insight into how we can be patient with others when he wrote the Colossian church saying he was praying and continually asking God to fill them "with the knowledge of his will through all the wisdom and understanding that the Spirit gives, so that you may live a life worthy of the Lord and please him in every way: bearing fruit in every good work, growing in the knowledge of God, being strengthened with all power according to his glorious might so that you may have great endurance and patience" (Colossians 1:9-11). It is by and through the glorious might of God that patience comes.

When I think of patience, waiting comes to mind. I am often not very good at waiting. Are you?

---

[4] Hymntime.com

William Henry Bellamy wrote the hymn "Wait, and Murmur Not," urging us to do everything we do without complaining as we wait, inferring patience, for the Lord's return and our eternal rest, echoing Hebrews 12:1-3.

"Therefore, since we are surrounded by such a great cloud of witnesses, let us throw off everything that hinders and the sin that so easily entangles. And let us run with perseverance the race marked out for us, fixing our eyes on Jesus, the pioneer and perfecter of faith. For the joy set before him he endured the cross, scorning its shame, and sat down at the right hand of the throne of God. Consider him who endured such opposition from sinners, so that you will not grow weary and lose heart."

Stanza 1
O troubled heart, there is a home
Beyond the reach of toil and care;
A home where changes never come:
Who would not fain be resting there?

This first stanza speaks to our troubled hearts and echoes the words of Jesus, "Do not let your hearts be troubled. You believe in God, believe also in me. My Father's house has many rooms; if that were not so, would I have told you that I am going there to prepare a place for you? And if I go and prepare a place for you, I will come back and take you to be with me that you also may be where I am" (John 14:1-3).

The toils and cares we face here on earth will never reach

this place prepared for Christ-followers that will never change. We must come to a saving knowledge of Jesus Christ to find and experience rest.

Refrain
O wait, meekly wait, and murmur not,
O wait, meekly wait, and murmur not
O wait, O wait,
O wait, and murmur not.

Because we know that "...The LORD is the everlasting God, the creator of the ends of the earth. He will not grow tired or weary, and his understanding no one can fathom" we can rest assured that He will give the weak strength and increase their power. We know that "those who hope in the LORD will renew their strength. They will soar on wings like eagles; they will run and not grow weary; they will walk and not be faint" (Isaiah 40:28-31). God works in us enabling us "to will and to act in order to fulfill his good purpose." Therefore, we are to "Do everything without grumbling or arguing" (Philippians 2:13-14).

Stanza 2
Yet when bowed down beneath the load
By Heav'n allowed, thine earthly lot;
Look up! thou'lt reach that blest abode;
Wait, meekly wait, and murmur not.

When we are heavily burdened, we must recognize the

sovereignty of God that directs and allows what happens. As we look to Jesus (Hebrews 12:1-2) we can cast our cares on Him (Psalm 55:22). We have the promise that God will enable us to endure whatever comes our way (1 Corinthians 10:13), so, we "wait for the LORD" (Psalm 27:14).

Stanza 3

Toil on, nor deem, tho' sore it be,
One sigh unheard, one prayer forgot;
The day of rest will dawn for thee;
Wait, meekly wait, and murmur not.

Keep toiling on even when it is painful. We know that God hears us (2 Samuel 22:7) and we look forward to the day of rest that we are promised (Revelation 14:13). We eagerly await the day of rest as we rest in Him and wait patiently for Him (Psalm 37:7).

Prayer: Heavenly Father, we are prone not to be patient and to murmur as we wait on You. Help us look to You and trust in You so that we can wait patiently for You. Thank You for the promise we have of eternal rest. In Jesus' name, Amen.

Thought for the Day: "The day of rest will dawn for thee; wait, meekly wait, and murmur not."

Day Five: God's Patience

By Harriet

Today's Bible Nugget

Zion is first mentioned in 2 Samuel 5:7 as a Jebusite hill fort captured by David's men that later became the city of David. When Solomon built the temple in Jerusalem, the word Zion became used for both places. Interestingly, in Zechariah 2:7, "Zion" is told to "escape Babylon." So here it refers to people who are in exile. Hebrews 12:18-22 follows Zechariah's train of thought. Zion is the people of God wherever they are—this is the restored Zion being assembled in heaven (the New Jerusalem) which will come down out of heaven to earth to a place on earth called Mt. Zion (Revelation 21). So, Zion is used to refer to both a place and a people; much like the word "church" refers to both a building and a people.

We've been talking about times when God seemed to work slowly in our lives, requiring us to learn patience as we wait on Him, but perhaps it would be good to think for a minute about all the times God has had to be patient with us. Can you think of times in your life when God was patient with you? If I pause and reflect on it for a while, I can think of many times in my life when I tried God's patience, yet He continued to walk near me, forgive me of the times I attempted to do things my way, and patiently allow me to learn that His ways are better.

When I think of God's patience with us, I think of how a parent is patient with a child. One of my four children had an independent spirit a mile wide. Sometimes he would be struggling to do something, like tie his shoes for example, and I would reach in to lend him a hand. I can still hear him snap, "I do it by self!" as he pushed my hands away… and yes, he would say "by self" instead of "by myself."

I used to attend a morning Bible study that had a preschool program. At the time, I had two preschoolers to get to their various classes, and this one always insisted on walking alone. I would reach down to try to grab his hand in hopes of keeping him more on task and less prone to wander after something—a butterfly on the path between the parking lot and church, perhaps—and he would pull his hand back and assert, "I walk by self."

My mother used to use the phrase, "My patience is growing thin." One of us kids tried to mimic this phrase as a child and mistakenly said, "My patience is getting skinny." Well, I think I have probably made God's patience "get skinny" more than once in my life as I tried to do things "by self," but, patient He remained.

In today's nugget we get a glimpse into God patiently building His church, from a small Jebusite hillside fort to a grand building in the form of the temple built by Solomon, to a people who love Him and worship Him today in many different buildings all over the world. And someday we will see God's finished work—His church that He built over centuries worshiping Him in the New Jerusalem. This church will be a people without sin. It will include us—purified, whole, and complete.

As wonderful as this is, God doesn't just work patiently with us in a corporate way. He works with us on an individual level too, patiently growing us every day of our lives into the person and people He created us to be.

One of my favorite verses about patience is Habakkuk 2:3, "For the vision is yet for an appointed time... though it tarry, wait for it; because it will surely come, it will not tarry" (KJV). This verse says so much to me about patience on both sides of the equation. The words were given to Habakkuk regarding a specific vision he had. They show that when God says something will happen you can be sure it will happen, but they also show that God's timing is not our timing. This wait that is sometimes included in God's perfect timing requires patience on both our part and God's. Isaiah 40:31 reminds us that, "they that wait upon the Lord shall renew their strength; they shall mount up with wings as eagles; they shall run, and not be weary; they shall walk, and not faint" (KJV).

Prayer: Heavenly Father, You are so patient with us. Thank You for all the times You have patiently loved us when we were unlovely, walked beside us when we were pulling away, not turned away from us when we were rebellious, and continued to bless us when we were undeserving. May we never forget Your patience and loving kindness toward us. In Jesus' name, Amen.

Thought for the Day: When God asks us to be patient, He is not asking anything of us that He does not exemplify Himself. He shows us how it's done.

Week Three:

Joy

Nuggets of Wonder from the Books of Poetry

Six books in the Old Testament are known as books of Poetry. These books, sometimes called the Books of Wisdom, are poems, songs, and wise sayings that the ancient Jews studied and used in their daily lives. Five of these books are clustered in the middle of the Old Testament, coming just before the books of prophecy. Lamentations is the exception—that little songbook is snuggled up next to Jeremiah in the Prophecy section.[5]

The six Books of Poetry in the Old Testament are: Job, Psalms, Proverbs, Ecclesiastes, Song of Songs (Song of Solomon), and Lamentations.

Fruit of the Spirit, Joy

This week the focus is on the fruit of the Spirit, joy. The Greek word *chara* which means our joy is based on our relationship with God. This joy is not the result of happenstance or our good circumstances, it is present and constant because of our relationship with God.

---

[5] Poetry and Wisdom Books of the Bible: The Beginner's Guide - OverviewBible accessed 8/3/22

"May the God of hope fill you with all joy and peace as you trust in him, so that you may overflow with hope by the power of the Holy Spirit" (Romans 15:13).

Day One: The Joy of Restoration

By Harriet

Today's Bible Nugget

Psalm 19 describes God's revelation to man in two volumes. Volume 1, found in verses 1 - 6, describes God's revelation in creation and Volume 2, verses 7-14, describes God's revelation to man through Scripture. There is a certain pattern to the poetry in verses 7 - 9 where the first line tells what something is, and the second line tells what it does. For example, verse 7 says, "The law of the Lord is perfect, restoring the soul." (What is it? It's perfect. What does it do? It restores the soul.)

During my childhood in Nigeria, we didn't throw anything away. Damaged metal barrels that our goods had shipped in that couldn't be reused to ship in again became flowerpots for roses which kept the ground insects like termites from damaging the cherished roses. We cut out pictures from old magazines and glued them to construction paper to make Valentines, birthday, and Christmas cards. We used old metal tins to make yard candles for nighttime outside activities, and of course our parents passed down clothes from one child to another, even from one family to another. But the Nigerians around us were perhaps even more creative and resourceful, using the rubber from old inner tubes to make slingshots, making old tires into shoes, tin cans into drinking cups, flour bags into handbags, and much more. These restored and repurposed items brought fresh joy to those using them.

Joy is closely linked to restoration in Scripture: Psalm 51:12 "Restore to me the joy of my salvation..." Isaiah 61:3 "To grant those who mourn in Zion, giving them a garland instead of ashes, the oil of gladness instead of mourning, the cloak of praise instead of a disheartened spirit..." (NASB), and Psalm 30:11 "You turned my wailing into dancing; you removed my sackcloth and clothed me with joy."

I never hear this last verse that I don't think of the story I've heard all my life of what happened at my birth. I was born in a remote jungle area in Nigeria. My parents were only there for one year while the missionary family normally stationed there was in America on furlough. This was one of the most remote, still quite wild, areas in Nigeria at the time. My dad used to tease me and tell me that I was dropped there by accident when the stork got the hiccups while on his way to Buckingham Palace with a little princess (me) in his beak. The true story of my birth is almost as interesting.

I was born in a small jungle hospital, delivered by my dad. Then Mom and I were transported to our home, where Mom would convalesce. The road from the hospital to home was dirt and long, so men carried Mom home on a stretcher. She lay on the stretcher holding sleeping me in her arms. Seeing us lying still and being carried like this, the people in the village thought we had both died and they began to wail and mourn. The men carrying Mom realized what the people thought, so they told Mom to sit up and wave to the people. She did this and she also held me up to show to them. Their mourning turned to dancing, like the verse says, as they sang, danced, clapped, and followed behind us in a joyous parade. They had thought we were dead, but we were alive. To the villagers, we had been restored.

When something gets restored, renewed, or revived it brings us great satisfaction and joy. This is especially true if what has been restored is a person. Have you known someone who was seriously ill and then made well again? In 2020 my then 90-year-old father contracted Covid and became quite sick. He was hospitalized and at one point we thought he was not going to make it. How we rejoiced when he recovered and was back home feeling normal again.

But all of this pales in comparison to the eternal joy experienced when a lost soul, once destined for hell, is restored through salvation. Jesus said in Luke 15:10 that even the angels in heaven rejoice when a sinner repents.

Prayer: Gracious Father, only You can truly restore a person. We pray for restoration through salvation for our loved ones who do not know You and we thank You for the joy that restoration brings. In Jesus' name, Amen.

Thought for the Day: Our hearts will abound in joy when we experience God's restorative touch.

Day Two: Joy to the World

By Shirley

Worship Hymn Focus
Joy to the World
1719 by Isaac Watts

From our understanding of who God is and what He has done, is doing, and will do for us in the future, we come to understand joy and how to cultivate and exhibit the fruit of joy in our own lives.

"Joy to the World," written by the prolific hymn writer, Isaac Watts, has Psalm 98:4-9 as its basis.

"Shout for joy to the LORD, all the earth, burst into jubilant song with music; make music to the LORD with the harp, with the harp and the sound of singing, with trumpets and the blast of the ram's horn— shout for joy before the LORD, the King. Let the sea resound, and everything in it, the world, and all who live in it. Let the rivers clap their hands, let the mountains sing together for joy; let them sing before the LORD, for he comes to judge the earth. He will judge the world in righteousness and the peoples with equity."

Although we think of this as being a Christmas Carol, Watts did not write this jubilant hymn to be sung only at Christmas. It is a joyful declaration praising Christ's coming to give His life as a sacrifice for our sin so we can be saved. He lived on earth as fully God and fully man, died upon the cross, was resurrected, and then returned to heaven, where He is now seated at the right hand of the throne of God. As Christ-followers we have the assurance that He will return someday and win the final victory over sin. What a great reason to be joyful!

Stanza 1

Joy to the world, the Lord is come!
Let earth receive her King;
Let every heart prepare Him room,
And heav'n and nature sing,
And heav'n and nature sing,
And heav'n, and heav'n, and nature sing.

We joyfully declare that "Christ Jesus came into the world to save sinners" (1 Timothy 1:15). The effects of His coming—to give His life as a sacrifice for our sin so we can be saved—are still experienced today. He also came to be our King (Matthew 2:2). In joyful response to the coming of our Savior and King, we gladly prepare our hearts to receive Him as we join the heavenly hosts and all of creation in singing His praises.

Stanza 2

Joy to the earth, the Savior reigns!
Let men their songs employ;
While fields and floods, rocks, hills, and plains
Repeat the sounding joy,
Repeat the sounding joy,
Repeat, repeat, the sounding joy.

Jesus Christ reigns now and for eternity as "both Lord and Messiah" (Acts 2:36). Mankind is to join creation in praising the Lord (Psalm 148:7-13). Because of who the Lord is and all that He has done for us, we can "Be joyful in hope" (Romans 12:12).

Stanza 3
No more let sins and sorrows grow,
Nor thorns infest the ground;
He comes to make His blessings flow
Far as the curse is found,
Far as the curse is found,
Far as, far as, the curse is found.

This stanza begins with the admonition for us to choose not to allow sins and sorrows to grow. It references Genesis 3 when the serpent tricked Eve into eating from the tree of the knowledge of good and evil. After Eve ate the fruit, she gave some to Adam who ate it also. Their sin brought about God's curse on them—and us (Romans 3:23). "But God demonstrates his own love for us in this: While we were still sinners, Christ died for us" (Romans 5:8) ending the reign and dominion of sin forever. "In him we have redemption through his blood, the forgiveness of sins, in accordance with the riches of God's grace" (Ephesians 1:7). God's blessings flow to us anywhere the effects of the curse are found.

Stanza 4
He rules the world with truth and grace,

And makes the nations prove
The glories of His righteousness,
And wonders of His love,
And wonders of His love,
And wonders, wonders, of His love.

Jesus "has gone into heaven and is at God's right hand—with angels, authorities and powers in submission to him" (1 Peter 3:22). He desires that all people hear the gospel so they will understand His righteousness and "see what great love the Father has lavished on us, that we should be called children of God! And that is what we are! The reason the world does not know us is that it did not know him" (1 John 3:1).

Prayer: Heavenly Father, thank You for the joy of salvation that came through Your Son Jesus. May I leap for joy and break out singing joyous praises to You as I experience His presence with me today and always. In Jesus' name, Amen.

Thought for the Day: Nothing brings more joy than knowing you are eternally secure in your relationship with Christ.

Day Three: Hallelujah, Praise the Lord!

By Harriet

Today's Bible Nugget

The word hallelujah is derived from three Hebrew words. *Hal* is from a word meaning praise, *el* from a word for the plural form of you, as in all of you; and *jah* is from the word that means God. Thus, hallelujah is a call to everyone to praise God. In the book of Psalms, chapters 146, 147, 148, and 149 all start with hallelujah or in some translations it might say, "Praise the Lord!" Then, in the last chapter of the book, chapter 150, every verse starts with this word or phrase. And the last verse of Psalms says, "Let everything that has breath praise the Lord!" – or Hallelujah!

That Sunday morning, someone sat in the pew that Mrs. S. had always considered hers. Mrs. S. knew the person, but not well. Didn't they know it was where she always sat? Mrs. S. slid in next to the woman. The pew was nearly full, so the woman had to scoot over to make room and still the two women almost sat on top of each other.

The first song started, and both women stood up and began to sing. It became apparent quickly that the two were trying to out-sing each other. One projected her voice loudly and the other would then increase her volume. And the pattern continued through the next several songs. After a break for announcements and the morning prayer, another song started. The women were ready. They both stood to their feet quickly and began to sing at the tops of their voices… only to discover to their horror and everyone else's amusement that it was the choir special.

This is a true story. I did not witness it myself but have heard my parents tell it many times. Mrs. S. was my parents' friend who later laughed as she retold the story herself. Fortunately for both of the women involved, God enjoys hearing His children praise Him, even if it's at a time when the world tells them they should remain quiet, like during the choir special.

This funny story may not be the best example of praising God. I suspect both women had their own pride and competitive spirits more in their minds than true worship. Praise isn't always through singing either, something for which I am thankful since I am not a good singer. Thankfully, the Bible only tells us to make a joyful noise, not an on-key, in-tune sound.

Praise comes in many forms, with singing as only one of them. True praise brings joy. Giving God thanks can be a form of praise, according to Psalm 106:1. Playing a musical instrument can be a way of expressing praise, according to Psalm 147:7. Ephesians 5:19 says that speaking about God can also be a way we praise Him, as can be prayer (1 Thessalonians 5:17), and clapping our hands (Psalm 47:1). The wise men fell to their knees in worship in Matthew 2:11

to show their praise of God, and the list could continue on and on. I'm sure you can think of others. What is the strangest situation in which you found yourself praising God?

Many years ago, the son of a close friend of mine landed in jail for a couple of days because of a minor issue. He was forced to show a police officer his license to prove his age, and when the police ran his card, it showed an unpaid ticket for a traffic violation. Because the young man had been rude to him, the policeman arrested him for the unpaid ticket. This was back before cell phones and the young man couldn't reach his parents, so he ended up using his one phone call to call me late on a Saturday night. That was the one and, so far, only time I have ever received a phone call from jail. I assured him I would keep trying to reach his mom and if I couldn't, I would post his bail the next day, but either way someone would be there to get him out of jail. I did get hold of his mom the next day, a Sunday, but his parents could not post his bail and get him until Monday morning.

His mother later shared her side of the experience with me. She said when she learned later that Sunday afternoon that her son was going to be spending a second night in jail, she sunk onto the floor and cried. But then she realized she could have gotten a far worse phone call. He could have been in jail under much worse circumstances, or she could have gotten a call from someone telling her that her son was dead. She said that realization had her praising God with sincere praise, and the more she praised God, the more she realized that all of it was completely and safely in His hands, and she said she began to be filled with joy over that truth.

Prayer: Heavenly Father, fill our hearts with praise, even and especially at times when we may be going through difficulties. Help us to remember that You have us and all we are concerned about safely in Your hands. In Jesus' name, Amen.

Thought for the Day: Praising God brings you joy, always.

Day Four: Joy Unspeakable

By Shirley

Worship Hymn Focus
Joy Unspeakable
1900 by Barney E. Warren

Happiness is the result of our perception that the things happening around us are positive. Joy, on the other hand, comes from God, and is the result of the indwelling of the Holy Spirit in the life of a Christ-follower as a fruit of the Spirit. When we come to Christ and begin learning about Him, we will choose to live a life of joy.

The degree to which joy manifests itself in and through a Christ-follower is directly proportionate to the amount of time they spend communicating with God (through prayer, Bible reading, studying, meditating, contemplating) and obeying Him.

We "rejoice in the Lord" (Philippians 4:4) because of who Jesus is, what He did for us on the cross, what He is doing for us presently, and what He will do for us in the future. Regardless of what is going on in our lives, God's joy resounds in our hearts because of our faith in Him.

Barney E. Warren wrote a wonderful hymn, "Joy Unspeakable," that describes the unspeakable joy Christ-followers can experience in their lives.

Stanza 1

I have found His grace is all complete,
He supplieth ev'ry need;
While I sit and learn at Jesus' feet,
I am free, yes, free indeed.

We are saved by grace through faith (Ephesians 2:8-9). "My grace is sufficient for you" from 2 Corinthians 12:9 promises that He supplies what we need. When we learn from God (John 6:45) we receive the blessings of grace (James 4:6). When we come to know the truth, "the truth will set [us] free (John 8:32).

Refrain

It is joy unspeakable and full of glory,
Full of glory, full of glory,
It is joy unspeakable and full of glory,
Oh, the half has never yet been told.

In the refrain we are again expressing that the joy of the Lord is so extraordinary that we are at a loss to describe it adequately. All of the words that have ever been spoken to describe the joy of the Lord have only scratched the surface in describing this joy!

Stanza 2

I have found the pleasure I once craved,
It is joy and peace within;
What a wondrous blessing! I am saved
From the awful gulf of sin.

Ecclesiastes 3:11 tells us that God "has also set eternity in the human heart." Don Richardson, in "Eternity in Their Hearts: Startling Evidence of Belief in One True God in Hundreds of Cultures Throughout the World,"[6] discusses how different cultures throughout the world show signs of yearning for God. We are grateful to have found the only thing that can fulfill that yearning—a relationship with Christ. Because of this relationship we have joy and peace within our hearts (Romans 15:13). We sing of the "wondrous blessing" of our salvation through which the gulf of sin is banished, and we are saved (Romans 10:9-13).

Stanza 3
I have found that hope so bright and clear,
Living in the realm of grace;
Oh, the Savior's presence is so near,
I can see His smiling face.

Having "been justified by his grace," we became "heirs having the hope of eternal life" (Titus 3:7). As Christ leads us further into "the realm of [His] grace," we learn to abide in the teaching of Christ (2 John 1:9), "with minds that are alert and fully sober," we "set [our] hope on the grace that comes when Jesus Christ is revealed" (1 Peter 1:13). We know He is always with us and that we are filled with the measure of all the fullness of God (Ephesians 3:19), just as if we could see

---

[6] Richardson, D. (2006). "Eternity in Their Hearts" Bethany House Publishers.

His smiling face.

Stanza 4
I have found the joy no tongue can tell,
How its waves of glory roll!
It is like a great o'erflowing well,
Springing up within my soul.

Because of our relationship with Christ, we are granted joy so incredible that we cannot really describe it with words. Through this relationship and God's Word we gain the knowledge of the glory of God (2 Corinthians 4:6)—not facts or information—but an experience and connection with Him. The indwelling Holy Spirit enables us to radiate His glory like "waves of glory." That "great o'erflowing well, springing up within [our] soul" allows us to experience the unspeakable joy of the Lord.

Prayer: Gracious Father, teach us to respond to Your greatness, power, presence, glory, mercy, and grace with joy. In Jesus' name, Amen.

Thought for the day: "The LORD is my strength and my shield; my heart trusts in him, and he helps me. My heart leaps for joy, and with my song I praise him" (Psalm 28:7).

Day Five: The Joy that Awaits Us

By Harriet

Today's Bible Nugget

Ecclesiastes 3:11 says that God has placed eternity in the human heart. The word for eternity is the Hebrew word *Olam.* It can be translated as "darkness," as in unable to be seen like in the future that is still unclear to us, or it can be translated as "forever." Most often the word as it appears in this verse is translated, "forever," and we take it to mean that God has placed an awareness that this life is not all there is, an awareness that there is something yet to come after we die. But even the translation that has us thinking about our "dark" or an unseen future makes me think of Psalm 139:12, which reminds us that darkness is not dark to God.

Forever is a long time. It spans all eternity from before time (as we measure it) began, to long after it ceases. That's what God has placed in our hearts, according to Ecclesiastes 3:11. In other words, He has placed an awareness within us that this life is not all there is. We instinctively know that there is another existence after we die. The question this God-given awareness brings is, where will we go after we die? Where will we spend our forever and what will it be like?

When we are young, with days ahead of us spreading out as far as our minds can imagine, a lifetime seems like a long time. When we cross about the fifth decade of our lives, however, and we have less days ahead of us than behind us, a lifetime seems short. But forever… now that's always a long time, no matter where on the spectrum of eternity we are.

My father-in-law died before I met my husband—killed instantly when a small twin engine plane he piloted crashed. He alone perished since he was the only person in the plane. My husband was only sixteen, and we did not meet until he turned twenty-two. Even though I never knew my father-in-law, I was blessed to know my mother-in-law and hear some of her wisdom through the years.

Regarding losing her husband, I once heard her say, "I learned in school that there is a place called Alaska, and I believed Alaska existed and was a real place. But I've never been there, so I can't say from experience that it exists. But then my brother got stationed in Alaska when he was in the military. Then I knew with certainty that it was a real place because I had a brother there."

After pausing for this to sink in to me and anyone else who may have been listening, she would add, "That's how I feel about heaven. I learned from the Scripture that it was a real place but had to believe it by faith alone until my husband was killed. Now I know with certainty it is a real place because my husband is there."

My mother-in-law knew her husband was in heaven because she had shared life with him and knew he was a believer, a Christ-follower. I don't want to be remiss by implying everyone goes to heaven after they die—they do not. Only those who have given their lives to Jesus, accepted His sacrifice on the cross for their sins, and have asked Him to be their Savior and Lord will spend eternity in heaven. This truth should give us a great burden for the lost and drive us to evangelism.

For those of us who believe, what will heaven be like? That question could be the topic of a study in itself. Whole books have been written about it. Will it have ever-expanding fields of the greenest grass we've ever seen? Will it have a city with streets of gold that we enter through pearly gates? It would truly require a thorough study of the Scripture as some authors have done, but sticking to this week's theme of joy, I will limit my observations about what heaven will be like to only one small aspect—there will be comfort and great joy in heaven. How do I know this? It can be found in many places in Scripture. In the space I have, I will share just a few.

Revelation 7:16-17 says, "Never again will they hunger; never again will they thirst. The sun will not beat down on them, nor any scorching heat. For the Lamb at the center of the throne will be their shepherd; he will lead them to springs of living water. And God will wipe away every tear from their eyes."

Psalm 68:3 says, "But the righteous shall be glad; they shall exult before God; they shall be jubilant with joy!" (ESV)

Luke 6:23 says, "Rejoice in that day and leap for joy, because great is your reward in heaven." And Luke 15:7

speaks of the great joy in heaven when a sinner repents.

The passage in Ecclesiastes that tells of God putting eternity in our hearts also assures us that God makes everything beautiful in its time. Though we may experience beauty in one form or another in this lifetime, it does not even begin to compare to the beauty we will know in heaven. Likewise, the joy we know now pales in comparison to the joy that awaits us in heaven.

Prayer: Heavenly Father, sometimes when we are facing heartache, difficulties, or loss, it's not easy to hold fast to the truth that joy awaits us in heaven. Help us in those times to know heaven is a real place and that it is our eternal destination if we have placed our faith in You. In Jesus' name, Amen.

Thought for the Day: Do you have a loved one in heaven? Can you say, like my mother-in-law, you know it is a real place now that you have a loved one there?

Week Four:

Nuggets of Wonder from the Major Prophets

A prophet in the Bible was someone who announced the declarations of God. The Hebrew word for prophet is *Nebi,* which is derived from an action verb that means "to bubble forth" like a fountain. The biblical prophets spoke truth that they received from God. Their unique vocation allowed them to speak authoritatively on God's behalf. They never spoke on their own authority, nor did they share their own opinions. They only shared their message as God instructed them.[7]

The Old Testament prophets are divided into those considered major, who had a greater, more profound impact, and minor, who also prophesied for the Lord but with a smaller or lesser reach or impact.

The four major prophets (and the books bearing their names) are: Isaiah, Jeremiah, Ezekiel, and Daniel.

Fruit of the Spirit, Peace

This week the focus is on the fruit of the Spirit, peace. The Greek word *eirene* encompasses harmony in our

---

[7] Who Were the Major and Minor Prophets in the Bible? (christianity.com) accessed 8/3/22

relationships with other people and God. This peace is the result of the indwelling Holy Spirit working in our hearts. It is not dependent upon our circumstances.

"The mind governed by the flesh is death, but the mind governed by the Spirit is life and peace" (Romans 8:6).

Day One: The Peace that Surpasses Understanding
By Harriet

Today's Bible Nugget

Have you ever felt like your work was all for naught, spending endless effort on a completely futile project? Take heart! Even the prophets had days like that. In Ezekiel 2:3-4, God tells Ezekiel, "I am sending you... to a rebellious nation.... The people to whom I am sending you are obstinate and stubborn." God continues in 3:7, "The people... are not willing to listen to you because they are not willing to listen to me." Yet, God told Ezekiel he was to speak God's words to the people whether they listened or not (Ezekiel 2:7). So, cheer up. You're in good company.

Years ago, I saw a cartoon comprised of several frames. In the first few frames an ant worked to build his anthill. One frame showed him carrying a small pile of sand on his back and the next showed him dumping his load onto the sandy ground. This was repeated a couple of times as the hill he built grew higher each time. But then a wave surged over the little hill and receded, leaving it flat, completely washed out. The last frame was a zoomed-out picture of a beach with a man in a beach chair near the ant who had apparently been watching. In that frame, the man speaks to the ant and says, "I've had days like that."

Yes, there really are beach ants in some places in this world. I wasn't sure, so looked it up before I retold this cartoon.

We've all had days like that, haven't we? Peace can feel elusive sometimes, especially on days like this when our work feels all for naught. This Bible nugget shows us that just because something we've put great effort into—investing time, prayers, physical labor, and often money—does not bring the result we had hoped for and perhaps even expected, our labor nevertheless has a purpose. God told Ezekiel the task he was to do would be in vain, but he was still told to do it. Speaking to a people who would not listen was still Ezekiel's God-given job, so we must conclude that the work itself had a purpose and value regardless of the outcome. This truth can help us attain peace, although others may not understand why we have that sense of peace.

This peace that others and sometimes even we cannot understand is referred to in Philippians 4:6-7 as the peace that passes understanding. In the English Standard Bible those verses read like this, "do not be anxious about anything, but in everything by prayer and supplication with thanksgiving let your requests be made known to God. And the peace of God, which surpasses all understanding, will guard your hearts and your minds in Christ Jesus."

These verses offers perspective as to what prompts that peace that we sometimes cannot understand—prayer and supplication with thanksgiving. Yes, it's possible to give thanks in every situation. It's not only possible; it's also something God specifically tells us to do in these verses in Philippians.

Back in early 1984, I suffered a miscarriage. I had found out I was pregnant just a week earlier with what would have been my second child. Shortly after finding out that news, I made a trip to a general merchandise store to pick up a few needed items. As I passed the baby section a warm feeling rushed over me because I had a secret—I was pregnant, something only I and my husband knew at the time. Then came the miscarriage. I thought I took it well emotionally and chalked it up to being so early in the pregnancy that it didn't feel like quite the loss it might have felt had I been further along. A couple of weeks later I made that same trek to the general merchandise store, something I did every few weeks to buy household supplies. This time when I walked past the baby section, a different emotion washed over me, and a flood of tears suddenly welled up in my eyes. I had to work hard to keep from falling completely apart right there in the store. My two-year-old sitting in the cart kept asking if I was okay. I assured him I was, but to tell the truth, my heart was breaking in a delayed reaction to my loss.

I got pregnant again more quickly than I had intended. That baby was not planned, but oh, so welcome. I carried that baby to term and have gotten to enjoy every day of his wonderful life. I am still enjoying watching him and his wife of twelve years now and the two precious grandchildren they have given me. I must confess I do not remember having the peace that passes understanding when I suffered that miscarriage. It was especially absent the day I had the meltdown in the store. But for many years now that episode in my life has brought me peace during other times when I faced hard, even tragic situations. It is an experience in my life where I saw firsthand that God is in control and purposeful in any event, no matter how challenging. He has His reasons. In the case of my miscarriage, His plan was for the other child to see life—a child who would never even have been conceived, much less born, lived, prospered, married, and given me grandchildren, if the baby I lost had been carried to term.

God is the author of peace, and He offers it abundantly to those who keep their eyes on Him and obey Him. I know from the task He gave Ezekiel that this peace is possible even when the work God gives a person to do seems fruitless, and I know from my own life that this peace is possible in times of great loss. A quote I've heard (I cannot find its origin) goes like this, "God is good all the time, and all the time God is good."

Prayer: Father, be near to us during frustrating or sad days in our lives. These will surely come, but Your peace abides forever. In Jesus' name, Amen.

Thought for the Day: God alone gives the peace that

surpasses understanding.

Day Two: It Is Well With My Soul

By Shirley

Worship Hymn Focus
It Is Well With My Soul
1873 by Horatio G. Spafford

Experiencing God's peace in our lives helps us gain a fuller understanding of not only how to experience that peace, but also how to cultivate and exhibit the fruit of peace in our own lives.

Christ-followers have peace with God through salvation, and we experience His peace which is beyond our ability to understand (Philippians 4:7). Christ Himself is our peace (Ephesians 2:14) and through His presence that brings peace in our lives, we can say, "It is well with my soul."

Horatio G. Spafford wrote the inspiring hymn, "It is Well With My Soul," after his four daughters, traveling with their mom on a ship that sank, drowned. Mrs. Spafford was found floating in the water and ten days later, sent a cable to her husband that said, "Saved alone."[8] This beautiful hymn testifies to the peace of God that we as Christ-followers can experience at all times—even in the midst of the most difficult circumstances.

---

[8] It Is Well with My Soul (hymntime.com) accessed 9/5/22.

Stanza 1

When peace, like a river, attendeth my way,
When sorrows like sea billows roll;
Whatever my lot, Thou hast taught me to say,
It is well, it is well with my soul.

God's peace flows over us like a gently flowing river. It transcends all understanding and guards [our] hearts and [our] minds in Christ Jesus" (Philippians 4:7), regardless of our current circumstances.

Refrain

It is well with my soul,
It is well, it is well with my soul.

By practicing what we "have learned or received or heard from [Paul] or seen in [him]" the God of peace will be with us and give us peace (Philippians 4:9) that leads us to proclaim boldly that all is well with our souls.

Stanza 2

Though Satan should buffet, though trials should come,
Let this blest assurance control,
That Christ hath regarded my helpless estate,
And hath shed His own blood for my soul.

We know the devil forcefully and repeatedly attacks us through various trials (1 Peter 4:12-13), yet we have the assurance that God is in control (Proverbs 19:21). This assurance is based on the "blood of the new covenant, which is shed for many for the remission of sins" (Matthew 26:28).

Stanza 3
My sin—oh, the bliss of this glorious thought!—
My sin, not in part but the whole,
Is nailed to the cross, and I bear it no more,
Praise the Lord, praise the Lord, O my soul!

We "were dead in trespasses and sins" (Ephesians 2:1), but He took all of our sin upon Himself and "made us alive together with Christ (by grace you have been saved)" (Ephesians 2:6). Oh, what a glorious thought. Christ "has taken [our sin] out of the way, having nailed it to the cross" (Colossians 2:14) and we do not bear that sin anymore because it is forgiven (Ephesians 1:7). Amen!

Stanza 4
For me, be it Christ, be it Christ hence to live:
If Jordan above me shall roll,
No pang shall be mine, for in death as in life
Thou wilt whisper Thy peace to my soul.

"Because of his great love for us, God, who is rich in mercy, made us alive with Christ even when we were dead in transgressions" (Ephesians 2:4-5). Here, the reference to the Jordan river seems to symbolize death. Yet, because we are alive in Christ, we will not experience the sting of death (Hosea 13:14). We can praise the Lord in life and in death (Philippians 1:19-21).

Stanza 5

But, Lord, 'tis for Thee, for Thy coming we wait,
The sky, not the grave, is our goal;
Oh, trump of the angel! Oh, voice of the Lord!
Blessed hope, blessed rest of my soul!

As we wait for Christ's return (1 Thessalonians 4:16) we are "preparing [our] minds for action, and being sober-minded, [setting our] hope fully on the grace that will be brought to [us] at the revelation of Jesus Christ when we will all hear His voice" (John 5:28-29).

Stanza 6

And Lord, haste the day when the faith shall be sight,
The clouds be rolled back as a scroll;
The trump shall resound, and the Lord shall descend,
Even so, it is well with my soul.

We know that faith "is confidence in what we hope for and assurance about what we do not see" (Hebrews 11:1). When we get to heaven, our faith will be replaced by sight as the clouds will roll back like a scroll (Isaiah 34:4). We are to live anticipating Christ's return (Revelation 22:12) when everyone will hear the trumpet sound (1 Corinthians 15:51-52) and see Him returning.

Prayer: Heavenly Father, thank You for Your presence which brings peace into our lives even when everything around us is in chaos. Help us learn to trust You more. In

Jesus' name, Amen.

Thought for the Day: "The peace of God, which transcends all understanding, will guard your hearts and your minds in Christ Jesus" (Philippians 4:7).

Day Three: The One Who Offers Peace

By Harriet

Today's Bible Nugget

What is God's Spirit like? Isaiah 11:2 gives us a great description of God's Spirit. This verse says, "And the Spirit of the Lord will rest on Him, (Jesus) The Spirit of wisdom and understanding, the Spirit of counsel and strength, the Spirit of knowledge and the fear of the Lord." So, what is God's Spirit like? It is full of wisdom, understanding, counsel, strength, and the knowledge and fear of the Lord. Wow! May God pour His Spirit out upon us!

I sometimes scroll certain social media sites to see friends who do not live near enough to see in person. I enjoy seeing their homes, families, and adventures. But these sites tend to be filled with advertisements that pop up repeatedly. They make me aware that people in today's world are always striving for something—the latest gadget, eternal youth, beauty, success, even peace of different types like world peace, financial peace, or personal peace. The Spirit of God offers peace and gives it freely. It is not something we have to strive to attain.

The peace God offers is given through His Spirit, whom Jesus called the Comforter in John 14 in the King James and some other versions of the Bible. This is the same Spirit of

God that is referred to in today's nugget, that is often called the Holy Spirit. Though the Isaiah passage does not mention peace in association with God's Spirit, other passages do.

John 14 is a sweet passage to read and meditate upon. In it, Jesus is telling His disciples that He will not be with them much longer. He promises to send them the Comforter and offers them peace. In John 14:27, Jesus tells them, "Peace I leave with you; my peace I give you. I do not give to you as the world gives. Do not let your hearts be troubled and do not be afraid."

This passage has special meaning to me. My high school had a tradition of singing these words to a certain tune at the last assembly of every year on what they called, "Move Up Day." Back then, my school was only comprised of three grades and only had three classes—Sophomore, Junior, and Senior classes. Each class sat in a specific section in the auditorium. Seniors sat in the front of the auditorium closest to the stage, Juniors in the back half of the auditorium, and Sophomores sat in the balcony. On Move Up Day, the Sophomores vacated their seats and moved to where the Juniors normally sat, leaving the balcony to be filled the next fall by the new class of Sophomores. Juniors moved to the front of the auditorium where they would sit as Seniors the next year, and the Seniors vacated their seats and stood against the walls encircling the seats. Then the Senior class all held hands and sang these words as their departing words to those who would remain behind them. What a bittersweet memory it is for me. It still stirs my emotions as I remember that last time saying goodbye to my school friends. Those in my class had been together for three years and in many cases longer, but we were about to go our separate ways forever.

How much more the disciples' hearts must have been touched by Jesus' words about His upcoming departure from them. In the case of my classmates, when we sang those words, we could only wish that those we had grown to love so much would experience peace. Oh, how different the words are coming from Jesus. He could, and did, actually leave His peace with His friends when He asked the Father to send them the Holy Spirit, who really can and does bring peace to believers.

When you are reading a novel, do you ever skip ahead and read the end before you finish the book? I must confess, I have done that on occasion. If the plot has taken me to a point of deep concern for a character that the author has gotten me to love, I have been known to look ahead to make sure that character is still alive at the end of the book. Knowing that the end turns out okay makes it easier for me to take the emotional rollercoaster that the plot might take me on. Well, we know how our story ends and how all creation ends if we've read God's Book. Spoiler alert: our story has a happy ending if we are followers of Jesus. God has it all in His hands and it will all work out for His glory and our good.

Prayer: Father, thank You for sending the Comforter to us.

Thank You for the peace He gives. In Jesus' name, Amen.

Thought for the Day: God gives us peace through His Spirit.

Day Four: Wonderful Peace

By Shirley

Worship Hymn Focus
Wonderful Peace
1889 by William D. Cornell and William G. Cooper

One of my many favorite Scripture verses is "Now may the Lord of peace himself give you peace at all times and in every way. The Lord be with all of you" (2 Thessalonians 3:16). As 2 Thessalonians is closing, the Apostle Paul pronounces a benediction and prayer for the Thessalonians. We take great comfort in knowing that Jesus Christ Himself gives us peace with God, in our hearts, and with others "at all times and in every way." He prays the presence of the Lord would be with them—all that any of us need. Because the Lord is with us, His presence brings peace in our hearts and in our relationships with each other.

The hymn, "Wonderful Peace," by Warren D. Cornell and William G. Cooper, speaks of the peace God gives His people. This peace, like a sweet melody, is a treasured gift from God that gives rest and looks forward to the eternal peace we will have in heaven.

Stanza 1
Far away in the depths of my spirit tonight
Rolls a melody sweeter than psalm;
In celestial-like strains it unceasingly falls

O'er my soul like an infinite calm.

When God gives us peace as a fruit of the Spirit, we experience peace very deep within our souls. Perhaps you speak of this as calmness or tranquility. This peace is like a beautiful melody that is sweeter than any psalm. In music, a series of notes creates the melody. God's peace has a heavenly-sounding melody that flows through us like an endless portion of calmness.

Refrain
Peace, peace, wonderful peace,
Coming down from the Father above!
Sweep over my spirit forever, I pray
In fathomless billows of love!

Once His work on earth was done, Jesus left us His peace that "will guard [our] hearts and [our] minds in Christ Jesus" (Philippians 4:6). We pray His peace will sweep over us forever in unending waves of love that calms and soothes our hearts.

Stanza 2
What a treasure I have in this wonderful peace,
Buried deep in the heart of my soul,
So secure that no power can mine it away,
While the years of eternity roll!

The "precepts of the LORD are right, giving joy to the

heart" (Psalm 19:8). As we yield our lives to God, His peace will be buried deep in the heart of our souls and keep us "in perfect peace" (Isaiah 26:3). God's peace is so certain that nothing or no one can ever take it away from us.

Stanza 3
I am resting tonight in this wonderful peace,
Resting sweetly in Jesus' control;
For I'm kept from all danger by night and by day,
And His glory is flooding my soul!

When the peace of God is present in our hearts, we find rest for our souls (Matthew 11:28-30). Because we are resting, trusting in Jesus' control, by faith we are protected by the power of God who "guards the course of the just and protects the way of his faithful ones" (Proverbs 2:8). Then His peace fills us with "an inexpressible and glorious joy" (1 Peter 1:8).

Stanza 4
And I think when I rise to that city of peace,
Where the Author of peace I shall see,
That one strain of the song which the ransomed will sing
In that heavenly kingdom will be:

The kingdom of God is a place of peace where God, the Author of peace, resides (1 Corinthians 14:33 KJV). Because of the peace we will experience with God in heaven, we will sing praises to Him (Revelation 5:8-12).

Stanza 5

Ah soul, are you here without comfort and rest,
Marching down the rough pathway of time?
Make Jesus your friend ere the shadows grow dark;
Oh, accept this sweet peace so sublime!

Remembering our spiritual deadness before we came to know Christ as Savior and Lord (Ephesians 2:1) spurs a desire in us to invite other people to share in God's peace (2 Corinthians 1:3-4). We want them to do what God commands so that they will be His friends (John 15:14), be "justified through faith," and "have peace with God through our Lord Jesus Christ" (Romans 5:1).

Prayer: Heavenly Father, thank You that we can have peace with You through our Lord Jesus Christ. In Jesus' name, Amen.

Thought for the Day: Are you experiencing the beautiful melody of God's peace flowing through you like an endless measure of calmness?

Day Five: The Cloud Rider

By Harriet

Today's Bible Nugget

In the Canaanite tradition, Baal is considered the rider of the clouds. He is called this in Canaanite religious texts. Thus, when Elijah ascended into the clouds in a chariot of fire, this was an insult to the Canaanites. It proved that Yahweh and His prophet were the real cloud riders. We see this truth again in other places in the Scripture. Isaiah 19:1 says, "A prophecy against Egypt: See, the LORD rides on a swift cloud and is coming to Egypt. The idols of Egypt tremble before him, and the hearts of the Egyptians melt with fear."

As a child I used to stretch out on a thick carpet of grass in the front yard of my tropical home, resting my head on a flat white painted rock. I'd lift my eyes up, searching the skies above me, watching the clouds float by. Sometimes I'd see only whiffs of clouds that seemed to travel across the sky in a hurry to get from one point to another. Other times large fluffy cotton-ball clouds sauntered slowly across the African sky, sometimes just hanging suspended in one place for hours. These filled my young mind with imagination. I'd picture myself sitting on one of those billowing clouds. Sometimes I built entire kingdoms in those cloud formations in my mind. Other times they were just my seat as I pictured myself passing by a friend who sat on a different cloud. Sometimes this imaginary me sitting up there on that cloud would attempt to jump to the cloud occupied by my imaginary friend. I'd wait until the two clouds floated close together and search for the best spots on each cloud to jump to and from.

As a child growing up in Africa in the 1960s, I spent many hours engaged in this activity. I lived in a time and a place with no television to watch, no electronic gadgets, and not even the newest toys to play with. Oh, I was not altogether alone. I had friends and activities with school, homework, church, and family-related things to occupy my time, but I had a lot of alone time, too. These times often found me laying my head on one of those flat white rocks that lined my dirt driveway and stretching my body out over the lush thick grass of my front yard. I'm not sure anything has felt more peaceful to me in my entire life since then, though sitting on an American beach as an adult watching waves wash ashore and then recede comes in a close second.

I have been a cloud-rider many times… in my imagination. But in real life, though I have flown through clouds and over them, I have never actually ridden on a cloud. The peace I felt as a child watching clouds and as an adult watching waves were not real peace, either. As a child in Africa, I lived during a time of war. My little home and mission compound may have been at peace, but the nation in which I lived split into two in a bloody civil war during my years there. Likewise, I've had peaceful vacation moments as an adult sitting on beaches watching waves, when, actually, my personal life was filled with financial uncertainty, concern for loved ones, uncertainty about upcoming changes, and other less than peaceful dynamics.

This temporal peace I felt contrasts with the real, eternal peace Jesus, the true rider of the clouds, brings. He offers us peace in our inner being now, and the day will come when He comes again and truly establishes peace for all eternity.

Isaiah, the same man who wrote the words quoted in today's nugget, spoke of this peace that Jesus will bring in a passage that we often hear at Christmastime, Isaiah 9:6-7a. These verses say, "For to us a child is born, to us a son is given, and the government will be on his shoulders. And he will be called Wonderful Counselor, Mighty God, Everlasting Father, Prince of Peace. Of the greatness of his government and peace there will be no end."

According to these verses and other places in Scripture, Jesus is the Prince of Peace, and He will bring a peace that will have no end. How amazing is that?

Prayer: Almighty Father, how we look forward to the day Jesus returns and establishes His eternal kingdom whose greatness and peace will never end. What a day that will be! Until then, keep our hearts in perfect peace as we wait for the day. In Jesus' name, Amen.

Thought for the Day: "Look, he is coming with the clouds, and every eye will see him...."

Week Five:

Kindness

Nuggets of Wonder from the Minor Prophets

There were twelve minor prophets and thus there are twelve minor prophet books in the Bible, each bearing the name of one of the prophets. The Major and Minor Prophets give us some of the richest glimpses and foreshadowing of Christ that we see in the entire Old Testament.[9]

The twelve books included in the Minor Prophets are: Hosea, Joel, Amos, Obadiah, Jonah, Micah, Nahum, Habakkuk, Zephaniah, Haggai, Zechariah, and Malachi.

Fruit of the Spirit, Kindness

This week the focus is on the fruit of the Spirit, kindness. The Greek word *chrestotes* means more than being nice. This kindness means moral goodness and integrity to discern the right thing to do, and the strength to choose to do the right thing.

"Be kind and compassionate to one another, forgiving each other, just as in Christ God forgave you" (Ephesians 4:32).

---

[9] Who Were the Major and Minor Prophets in the Bible? (christianity.com) accessed 8/3/22

Day One: What Does God Consider Good?

By Harriet

Today's Bible Nugget

Most of the book of Micah is a prophecy against evil. But in the middle of the book—in the midst of Micah's outcry against the wickedness of his time—he tells us what is good. In stark contrast to the evil of his day, Micah lists for us what God considers good in Micah 6:8 when he writes, "He has told you, mortal one, what is good; And what does the Lord require of you but to do justice, to love kindness, and to walk humbly with your God?" (NASB).

Some years ago, I knew a young man in my church who struggled with some mental health issues. At times this struggle was manifested in bouts of depression. Over time, with help from counseling and medication, this young man's depression lifted, and his overall mental health became much more stable. But during one of the times when he was feeling particularly depressed, my pastor reached out to him though a phone call. It was just a simple gesture of checking on someone through a phone call, but for this young man, the call came at just the right time and meant the world to him. I learned of this phone call years later when my pastor developed pancreatic cancer and after a couple of years with it, died. The funeral home that his family used had a web page where people could leave thoughts about him. This young man wrote about that time in his life when he was feeling "really down," as he put it, and the pastor called him. He said it was encouraging to him to realize someone cared about him.

It was just a simple act of kindness. It took almost no effort and only a few minutes, but it left an impression that will last a lifetime.

Being kind benefits others and makes the world a better place. That truth is something that seems obvious, but did you know that according to Proverbs 11:17, being kind to others benefits the person who is showing the kindness, too? The exact Scripture in the NIV says, "Those who are kind benefit themselves, but the cruel bring ruin on themselves."

How can being kind to another person also benefit the one showing kindness?

The answers to that question are myriad. For one thing, showing kindness to another requires that you get your focus off yourself and notice what someone else is going through, what they are struggling with. Having an other-oriented focus rather than a self-oriented focus helps us gain perspective. More often than not, we come away from our interactions with those other people to whom we are showing kindness to discover that our problems are not as bad as perhaps we had once thought they were. Showing kindness to others or even animals reduces stress in general and lifts a person's overall feelings of wellbeing. Some studies have shown that it may even increase a person's lifespan. And according to our highlighted Bible nugget in Micah 6:8, it is one of the three things that God has specifically said was good—to do justice, to show kindness, and to walk humbly.

Walking humbly can be challenging in our world today. We feel drawn to at least put our best foot forward on social media sites and often this crosses over to our engaging in self-promotion. We're all trying to earn a living, after all, and promoting what we do, or sell, is not only considered appropriate in today's world, in some instances our bosses expect this from us. Walking humbly may be a difficult thing to accomplish these days but showing kindness shouldn't be. It doesn't take much to be kind; sometimes all it takes is a phone call.

Prayer: Heavenly Father, You have shown us so much kindness. Everything we have and ever will have are gifts from You. The very air we breathe is from You and the ability to take another breath is only by Your will. Open our eyes to the needs of those around us and remind us that nothing we think we own is ours. We are just stewards of it for a short time. Create in us a heart of kindness and generosity. In Jesus' name, Amen.

Thought for the Day: God is so kind to us, let's not fail to extend that kindness to others.

Day Two: He Lifted Me

By Shirley

Worship Hymn Focus
He Lifted Me
1905 by Charles H. Gabriel

God's kindness to us gives us a fuller understanding of how to cultivate and exhibit the fruit of kindness in our own lives. The kindness of God is seen through His grace and mercy and "is intended to lead [us] to repentance" (Romans 2:4). When God sent Jesus to pay the penalty for our sins on the cross and bring us into relationship with Him, we could see His kindness.

The marvelous hymn, "He Lifted Me," written by Charles H. Gabriel reminds us of the account in Scripture of Peter getting out of the boat to go to Jesus and walking on the water. Fear overcame him when he noticed the strong wind and he began sinking. He cried out for Jesus to help him. Jesus reached out and saved him.

Before coming to the saving knowledge of Christ, we were sinking in our sin. Instead of facing possible drowning like Peter, our threat is eternal punishment.

Stanza 1
In loving-kindness Jesus came,
My soul in mercy to reclaim,
And from the depths of sin and shame

Through grace He lifted me.

Through God's kindness, love, and grace He lifts us out of the depths of our sin and shame. Titus 3:4-7, "when the kindness and love of God our Savior appeared, he saved us... through the washing of rebirth and renewal by the Holy Spirit, whom he poured out on us generously through Jesus Christ our Savior, so that, having been justified by his grace, we might become heirs having the hope of eternal life."

Refrain
From sinking sand He lifted me,
With tender hand He lifted me;
From shades of night to plains of light,
Oh, praise His Name, He lifted me!

The resounding refrain is our declaration of praise for what our God did for us through His Son Jesus. He "made us alive with Christ even when we were dead in transgressions" and "He raised us up with Christ and seated us with him in the heavenly realms in Christ Jesus, in order that in the coming ages he might show the incomparable riches of his grace, expressed in his kindness to us in Christ Jesus" (Ephesians 2:4-7).

Stanza 2
He called me long before I heard,
Before my sinful heart was stirred,
But when I took Him at His word,

Forgiv'n, He lifted me.

Thinking of God's forgiveness reminds us to praise Him "who has blessed us in the heavenly realms with every spiritual blessing in Christ. For He chose us in Him before the creation of the world to be holy and blameless in His sight. In love he predestined us for adoption to sonship through Jesus Christ, in accordance with his pleasure and will—to the praise of his glorious grace, which he has freely given us in the One he loves" (Ephesians 1:3-6). From God's Word we learn who He is and how He forgives when we confess of our sin and repent. When we come to Him and confess our sin "he is faithful and just and will forgive us our sins and purify us from all unrighteousness" (1 John 1:9).

Stanza 3
His brow was pierced with many a thorn,
His hands by cruel nails were torn,
When from my guilt and grief, forlorn,
In love He lifted me.

Jesus experienced numerous indignities on Golgotha at the hands of the soldiers. "They stripped him and put a scarlet robe on him, and then twisted together a crown of thorns and set it on his head" (Matthew 27:28-29). We know they nailed His hands and feet to the cross. "He himself bore our sins" in His body on the cross, so that we might die to sin and live for righteousness; "by his wounds you have been healed" (1 Peter

2:24). In the kindness of this healing, He lifted us out of the mire of our sin and guilt.

Stanza 4
Now on a higher plane I dwell,
And with my soul I know 'tis well;
Yet how or why, I cannot tell,
He should have lifted me.

As Christ-followers, God has "raised us up with Christ and seated us with him in the heavenly realms in Christ Jesus" (Ephesians 2:6). Our soul knows everything is well because we have "the peace of God, which transcends all understanding" (Philippians 4:7). We acknowledge that we cannot fully understand God's ways and why He would show His kindness toward us by sending His Son to earth to save those who believe in Him. Yet, through faith, we are established in His love, we are able to understand the kindness and love of Christ (Ephesians 3:17-18), and we trust Him to lift us out of our sin.

Prayer: Heavenly Father, thank You for Your kindness that led us to repentance and brought us into relationship with You. As we acknowledge Your kindness, enable us to exhibit the fruit of kindness in our lives. In Jesus' name, Amen.

Thought for the Day: "Now on a higher plane I dwell, and with my soul I know 'tis well." – Charles H. Gabriel

Day Three: More Powerful than Compulsion
By Harriet

Today's Bible Nugget

"This is the word of the LORD to Zerubbabel, saying, 'Not by might, nor by power, but by my Spirit,' says the LORD of hosts" (Zechariah 4:6). This is a well-known passage, but who was Zerubbabel? He was from the line of David (1 Chronicles 3:1-19). Thus, he was in the royal line and had the authority to sit on David's throne, but because Israel had been captured by Persia in his day, instead of being a king, Zerubbabel was a governor. He worked with the priest Joshua (or Jeshua) to rebuild the temple (Ezra 5:2), and he was named in the genealogy of Jesus, too! (Matthew 1:12)

"You can attract more flies with honey than with vinegar."

"Carrot or stick?"

These are two expressions that refer to the same thing—rewards versus punishments, or in other words, getting a desired response or action from a person or animal through either kindness that entices compliance, or force—often painful force. Both expressions appear to come out of rural America's country life. Carrot or stick specifically refers to getting a donkey or horse to go where you want them to by either hitting their behind parts with a stick or holding a carrot in front of their noses that they will willingly follow. Can you picture in your mind a sketch most of us have seen where a man rides a donkey? He's holding a fishing pole-like stick in his hand with a carrot on the end, continually dangling in front of the donkey's nose.

When I was a child, my grandfather lived on a farm and taught me to ride horses. I learned to put one foot in a stirrup and hoist myself up onto a saddle. I learned to hold the reins and how to pull one side tighter than the other to direct the horse to turn one way or the other. I also learned to use a short switch to smack the horse's backside if I wanted him to trot faster. I hated using that switch and consequently I usually just settled for plodding along slowly. Grandaddy always assured me that it didn't really hurt the horse much—it only stung him a little. Grandaddy said the horse was trained by it, so he was used to it, but I still hated using it.

As an adult when I became a mother and also a substitute teacher, I discovered that using rewards (carrots) instead of punishments (sticks) was still my preferred method of trying to motivate children under my care. It appears the Scripture sides with me. In today's nugget God tells Zerubbabel that His Spirit is more powerful than might or power according to the world's definition of power.

God's Spirit is multi-faceted. We looked at some of those facets in a previous verse and devotion in this book. That verse, Isaiah 11:2, mentioned wisdom, understanding, counsel, strength, knowledge, and the fear of the Lord. We are also looking at what the Bible calls the Fruit of the Spirit throughout this entire book. These are also facets of God's Spirit and among them is kindness. Kindness is the carrot that is stronger than the stick of trying to force something by one's own power. Colossians 3:12 tells us that as God's chosen people we should "clothe [ourselves] with compassion, kindness, humility, gentleness and patience."

What kinds of things does the world consider powerful? A person with a strong athletic body who wins games for someone's favorite team is sometimes called a powerful player. Politicians who make laws that people must obey are considered powerful. We have had dictators in our world who were considered powerful people. The very lives of the people in their countries depended on their whims. Sometimes these people even upset the entire world like Adolf Hitler tried to do.

Charles Schwab, a 1900s American steel manufacturer who was once considered a rich and powerful man, once said, "Kindness is more powerful than compulsion." Yes, Mr. Schwab, indeed it is. But it is only one small aspect of an all-powerful God's power.

Prayer: Heavenly Father, when we are feeling powerless in our lives may we remember that we serve You, an all-powerful God. Make Your spirit to rest upon us and manifest Itself through us in many ways, including kindness. In Jesus' name, Amen.

Thought for the Day: Your kindness to others is more powerful in its effect on them than you may ever realize.

Day Four: Bringing in the Sheaves

By Shirley

Worship Hymn Focus
Bringing in the Sheaves
1874 by Knowles Shaw

We are able to exhibit the fruit of kindness because of the riches of God's kindness that we experience through our relationship with Christ and our understanding through the Holy Spirit-inspired Word of God.

Kindness is a choice we make that shows in and through our words and actions. We are able to be kind because of the love and kindness God has shown us. We are to "be kind and compassionate to one another, forgiving each other, just as in Christ God forgave [us]" (Ephesians 4:32).

God does not show kindness to us and save us because we deserve it, and we do not show kindness to others because they deserve it. We show kindness to others because God was kind to us through His mercy and saved us (Titus 3:4-5).

A stately hymn we usually relate to evangelism is "Bringing in the Sheaves." This hymn reminds us that our response to the kindness of God who brought us salvation is to show kindness to others by sharing the Good News with everyone. We sing of sowing or planting seeds of the Word of God (Luke 8:11) whereby the Holy Spirit brings in the harvest of individuals (Luke 8:15) coming to a saving knowledge of Jesus Christ as their Savior and Lord.

Stanza 1
Sowing in the morning, sowing seeds of kindness,
Sowing in the noontide and the dewy eve;
Waiting for the harvest, and the time of reaping,
We shall come rejoicing, bringing in the sheaves.

As Christ-followers we are to make disciple-makers (Matthew 28:18-20) wherever we go throughout each day. We are to keep sharing the Good News that we know (2 Timothy 2:2) with all those whom God brings across our paths. The seeds of kindness we sow are the result of our relationship with Christ, following His example, and being obedient to His Word. Our goal in sharing God's Word is our trust in the work of the Holy Spirit to bring about conviction of sin and repentance in the hearts of those who experience the kindness of God.

Refrain
Bringing in the sheaves, bringing in the sheaves,
We shall come rejoicing, bringing in the sheaves;
Bringing in the sheaves, bringing in the sheaves,
We shall come rejoicing, bringing in the sheaves.

As we go about sowing seeds of kindness and God's Word, with all the saints we shall rejoice in the harvest of Christ-followers the Lord brings.

Stanza 2
Sowing in the sunshine, sowing in the shadows,
Fearing neither clouds nor winter's chilling breeze;
By and by the harvest, and the labor ended,
We shall come rejoicing, bringing in the sheaves.

As we live our lives, whether everything is going smoothly or we are in the throes of extremely difficult circumstances, we are to continue sharing the Good News with whomever we meet (Mark 16:15). We can share the Good News because God has told us not to be distressed by anything that is going on around us because He "will uphold [us] with [His] righteous right hand" (Isaiah 41:10). We are to sow continually the seeds of God's Word because a time is coming when we will not be able to work (sow) any longer.

Stanza 3
Going forth with weeping, sowing for the Master,
Though the loss sustained our spirit often grieves;
When our weeping's over, He will bid us welcome,
We shall come rejoicing, bringing in the sheaves.

While we may be cognizant of the command to share the Word of God with others, we sometimes fail to approach our sharing with a deep burden for the lost coming to Christ—a burden so deep that it causes us to weep. Also, at times we may grieve because we do not see the harvest we hoped to see. Throughout our lives we must remember that in "whatever [we] do, work at it with all [our] heart, as working for the Lord, not for human masters" (Colossians 3:23). Since we have faithfully served Him, we will be welcomed into heaven (Matthew 25:23). Along with God's harvest of believers, we will rejoice and praise Him for eternity" (Matthew 25:46).

What a glorious day it will be when we celebrate this harvest of believers with all the saints in heaven.

Prayer: Heavenly Father, thank You for Your kindness that saved and renewed us. May we show kindness in our actions and words to those whom You bring across our paths so that they will come to know You and Your saving grace. In Jesus' name, Amen.

Thought for the Day: How are you sowing seeds of kindness and the Word of God?

Day Five: What Message Are You Bringing?

By Harriet

Today's Bible Nugget

The last book in the Old Testament is Malachi. Not much is known of its author and in fact, it is not clear if the author's name was Malachi or if he was just an unknown prophet since the Hebrew word Malachi means "My [God's] messenger." Most of the book contains passages rebuking the people for their failures. But the last chapter tells of a coming day of the Lord. This day will be a terrible day for some (Malachi 4:5). But for those who fear God's name it will be a day of restoration when "the sun of righteousness will rise with healing in its wings" and the people will go forth skipping like calves from the stall.

"God's Messenger." That's what Malachi means. Are you and I Malachis? What message are we bringing to the world? Our world receives many messages from many places. Advertisements, songs, books, movies, television programs, news reports, magazines, all give messages to us. We are flooded with information and others' points of view in our lives today in ways the world has never experienced before. So many of these messages are harsh, even heartbreaking, yet our world is desperate to hear good news. Are we sharing good messages to people around us? If others know we are Christians they will look at our words, actions, and lifestyles and will get messages about God from them. What message are we giving? Is it a message of kindness?

As a young man, my husband John found himself put on the board of trustees of a well-respected, well-known, large seminary. He soon became embroiled in a great controversy because of the things the school was teaching at that time. One of the first gatherings he was asked to attend was a dinner with the faculty, and I was also invited. We sat at the table with a female member of the seminary administration whom John knew. Her husband had been one of John's high school teachers and his baseball coach. John used to babysit their children. Somehow the question of how a person is saved came up. This administrator did not believe that Jesus was the only way to heaven. In response to John's assertion that apart from Jesus a person would go to hell she exclaimed, "Why John. If we really believed that we would be knocking on doors trying to tell everyone about Jesus."

Years ago, I became friends with an unsaved person through an activity my child and her child both participated in. Due to my youth and inexperience, I was not comfortable sharing the gospel so instead I simply told her about my upbringing as a missionary kid and my current church involvement. Her mother had cancer and one afternoon, I got a phone call from my friend telling me her mom was in the hospital facing death. She said no one in her family attended church so she didn't know a preacher to call but thought I might. Instead of sending my preacher, I sent my husband John. That night in the hospital room, he shared the plan of salvation and my friend, her mother, and her sister all accepted Christ as their Savior. Her mother passed away a few weeks later and to this day, many years later, my friend still thanks me for sending John to share the gospel with them. My friend has the reassurance that her mother is in heaven, a reassurance she would not have had if John had not told them the good news of Jesus' love for sinners and His death on the cross to take away their sins.

Kindness dictates that we share the gospel to a lost world. The story of God's great love for us is the kindest message we can share with a lost and hurting world.

Prayer: Father, make us Your messengers. Open our mouths to share the good news of Your gift of Jesus to this lost world. Bring opportunities our way to share the gospel with others and give us the courage to do it. In Jesus' name, Amen.

Thought for the Day: What message are you bringing to the hurting and confused world around you? Telling others about Jesus is the kindest message you can speak.

New Testament

"Kingdoms of the world are based on a love of power, but God's kingdom is based on the power of love." – Dr. Peter Gentry, Franklin Street Sunday school class, 2019

The New Testament tells of a new covenant God makes with His people—a covenant of love. We see this stated plainly in John 13:34 where Jesus said, "A new commandment I give you: love one another. As I have loved you, so you must love one another."

Week Six:

Goodness

Nuggets of Wonder from the Gospels

The first four books of the New Testament are known as the Gospels. They are narratives covering the life and death of Jesus. The word gospel is derived from the Anglo-Saxon term *god-spell*, meaning "good story" or "good news."[10]

The gospels were written by four disciples whose names are also the titles of the books. These disciples and hence book titles are: Matthew, Mark, Luke, and John.

Fruit of the Spirit, Goodness

This week the focus is on the fruit of the Spirit, goodness. The Greek word *agathosune* which means expressing kindness or doing what is good. I've heard it defined as fierce kindness, doing the good and right thing even when it is hard.

"I myself am convinced, my brothers and sisters, that you yourselves are full of goodness, filled with knowledge and competent to instruct one another" (Romans 15:14).

---

[10] Gospel | Definition, History, & Facts | Britannica accessed 8/3/22

Day One: The Earth, an Example of God's Goodness
By Harriet

Today's Bible Nugget

The Gospel of Matthew contains many mountains. These include the mountain where Jesus was tempted (Matthew 4:1-11), the mountain where He gave the Sermon on the Mount (Matthew 5:1-16), the mountain where He fed the multitudes with only five loaves and two fish (Matthew 15:29-39), the Mount of Transfiguration (Matthew 17:1-9), the Mount of Olives where He told of His second coming, sometimes called the Olivet Discourse (Matthew 24:1-31), and in the very last verses of the book, from a mountain, Jesus claims all authority in heaven and earth and sends His disciples into the whole world in a passage known as the Great Commission (Matthew 28:16-20). The Gospel of Matthew portrays the Lord Jesus as the sovereign king. He is the Man of the mountain who can move mountains.

Psalm 33:5 (NKJV) says, "The earth is filled with the goodness of the LORD." I have been blessed to see some of this goodness in my childhood country of Nigeria. There was one town in particular where my denomination had a mission hospital, so from time to time, my parents went there to relive the staff. Both of my parents were medical professionals—

Dad was a physician and Mom a nurse. Though we were stationed at a different mission hospital in a different town, every now and then we ventured a little north to this town to help out. Located just outside its mission hospital compound stood an amazing rock mountain. My siblings and I loved to climb it. How I remember those adventures.

There was very little vegetation since the entire mountain consisted of large rocks of varying sizes, but I once saw a small crevice with a little dirt where a single large plant grew. The older friends who led our little group scared me by saying it was a "man-eating plant." They cautioned against touching it, claiming it might eat a finger. I know now it was some type of carnivorous plant that ate insects, and perhaps small rodents, but not people. Its method of eating something was to close around it and then dissolve that insect or small rodent in a solution it produced that poisoned and eroded them much like an acid would. But at the time I thought it would snap shut and cut my finger off if I touched the blossom, which did sort of resemble an open mouth. I marveled that such a plant existed and worried I might accidently run into something like it at any given moment in my life and touch it or stumble into it without realizing what it was. Still, it amazed me, and the view from near the top of that rock mountain filled me with wonder. I have never seen anything that compares to those rock mountains in my entire life since.

There were other treasures in Nigeria, too. Mom had Daddy stopped the car once so we could get out and see some beautiful orchids growing wild by the side of the dirt road we were on. In northern Nigeria precious and semi-precious stones could sometimes be found just lying on the ground by the careful eye of a child searching for such things. Amethyst crystals were particularly abundant. I still have one stuffed away in a drawer for safekeeping, that I got from a childhood friend who found it on the ground in northern Nigeria. Ikogosi, another town to the east of us, had a natural warm spring. Today it has been made into a resort with the warm spring flowing into a swimming pool used by the resort. Back then, my denomination had a Christian campground in Ikogosi with a chapel and a few cabins. We also had the warm water flowing into a much smaller swimming pool our mission had built. The Niger River runs through another part of this beloved country of my birth. That part of the country is in the tropical rain forest. It has suffered through the years because it is rich with oil and has been fought over and ravaged to some degree for this natural resource, but my memories of it from the early 1960s are almost magical. I can still see the thick jungle trees and hear monkey chatter all around me in my mind if I think back to that place and that time.

My experiences from my childhood in Africa are examples of the goodness of God in the beauty of the world. And America is just as beautiful. There's nothing in the world better than Kentucky, where I live now, in the autumn when the trees are all showing off their colors.

The astounding beauty of the world God has given us to live in is just one of the ways He fills His earth with His goodness—trees that bear delicious fruit and nuts and the ground He fills with vegetation for us to eat as well as rain to water them and sunshine to make them grow are examples of His goodness to us. Often people work the land to produce food, but where I live blackberries grow wild. I have a few favorite picking spots and every summer, in early July, I fill bowls and buckets with them to eat fresh, cook in yummy baked goods, or freeze for later. The earth is full of God's goodness, indeed.

Prayer: Gracious Father, You are so good to us. You pour out Your goodness on us and fill our earth and our lives with good things. May we never forget to thank You. In Jesus' name, Amen.

Thought for the Day: Do you want to see God's goodness? Just open your eyes and look around.

Day Two: Praise to the Lord, the Almighty

By Shirley

Worship Hymn Focus

Praise to the Lord, the Almighty

1680 by Joachim Neander

The goodness of God helps us gain a fuller understanding of how to cultivate and exhibit the fruit of goodness in our lives.

God is good, and He chooses to do good things and give us good things (James 1:17). A handwritten note in the margin of my Bible beside Galatians 5:22 says "goodness is the blessing and bounty of God."

Joachim Neander wrote the hymn "Praise to the Lord, the Almighty" that reminds us of all the ways we see and experience the goodness of God in His authority, providence, in creation, and salvation.

Stanza 1

Praise to the Lord, the Almighty, the King of creation!
O my soul, praise Him, for He is thy health and salvation!
All ye who hear, now to His temple draw near;
Praise Him in glad adoration.

We praise the Lord because He is the Almighty, the King of creation (Genesis 1:1). It is through Him that we have our health and salvation. Because "the LORD is in his holy temple; the LORD is on his heavenly throne" (Psalm 11:4) we are to draw near to Him who alone is worthy of our praise (Revelation 5:12).

Stanza 2
Praise to the Lord,
who o'er all things so wondrously reigneth,
Shelters thee under His wings, yea, so gently sustaineth!
Hast thou not seen how thy desires e'er have been
Granted in what He ordaineth?

We praise the Lord because He reigns over and controls everything in the universe (Psalm 96:10-13). God gives us shelter under His wings (Psalm 91:4), sustains us, and holds everything in the universe together (Colossians 1:17). We have seen with our own eyes how God providentially provides for our needs as He gives "every good and perfect gift" (James 1:17).

Stanza 3
Praise to the Lord,
who doth prosper thy work and defend thee;
Surely His goodness and mercy here daily attend thee;
Ponder anew what the Almighty can do,
If with His love He befriend thee.

We praise the Lord because of what He does for us. Because "he is [our] rock and salvation; he is [our] fortress, [we] will never be shaken" (Psalm 62:2). As we experience

God's goodness and mercy in our daily lives, we praise Him (Psalm 145:9), since we are His friends if we keep His commandments and remain in His love (John 15:10-14).

Stanza 4
Praise to the Lord, who,
when tempests their warfare are waging,
Who, when the elements madly around thee are raging,
Biddeth them cease, turneth their fury to peace,
Whirlwinds and waters assuaging.

The Lord has done so much for us that is worthy of praise. I am reminded of the account in Scripture where Jesus and His disciples were in a boat when a bad storm caused the waves to come up over the boat. Jesus was sleeping but woke up and calmed the storm for the frightened disciples. In the same way that Jesus calmed the storm and rescued the panicking disciples, He rescues us when we are experiencing the raging fury of our sin.

Stanza 5
Praise to the Lord, who, when darkness of sin is abounding,
Who, when the godless do triumph, all virtue confounding,
Sheddeth His light, chaseth the horrors of night,
Saints with His mercy surrounding.

Even though we may experience temporary delight in our sin, this delight will only last a moment (Job 20:5). When it seems like the godless are succeeding, we "rest in the LORD and wait patiently for Him" (Psalm 37:7). When Jesus, "the light of all mankind" came, His "light shines in the darkness and the darkness [does] not overcome it" (John 1:4-5). "...his mercies never come to an end" (Lamentations 3:22).

Stanza 6
Praise to the Lord, oh, let all that is in me adore Him!
All that hath life and breath,
come now with praises before Him;
Let the Amen sound from His people again,
Gladly for aye we adore Him.

The Lord is worthy of our praise, so "...all that is within me" praises Him. We invite all of creation to join us in singing praises to Him (Psalm 148:7-13). Because we "love the Lord [our] God with all [our] heart and with all [our] soul and with all [our] mind" (Matthew 22:37), we express our praise to Him and proclaim, "Blessed be the Lord, the God of Israel, from everlasting to everlasting! And let all the people say, 'Amen!' Praise the Lord!" (Psalm 106:48).

Prayer: Almighty Father, we praise You for all the ways we see and experience Your goodness. As we recognize Your goodness, may we respond by proclaiming Your praises. In Jesus' name, Amen.

Thought for the Day: The goodness and mercy of God are always with us.

Day Three: God's Good Gift of Salvation

By Harriet

Today's Bible Nugget

God spoke these words at Jesus' baptism, "This is my Son, whom I have chosen; listen to him"(Luke 9:35). The Jews present would recognize them as words from Old Testament passages. "This is my Son" was written in Psalm 2:7, "In whom I am pleased" comes from Isaiah 42:1, and "Listen to him" comes from Deuteronomy 18, where God explains that a true prophet should be listened to because what he says will happen.

There are people who have powerful testimonies about their salvation. They tell of terrible habits and temptations that once had a hold on them, and they share how Jesus saved them and brought them out of their sins. I do not have such a testimony. I accepted Jesus as a child sitting in the chapel of the seminary in Ogbomoso, Nigeria, during the mission's annual Vacation Bible School. I remember the moment clearly and I have never once questioned my salvation experience. I knew I was a sinner who needed forgiveness and understood that apart from turning to Jesus and praying to ask Him to forgive my sins and become my Savior, I would not enter heaven when I died.

I might not have a unique story to tell about my salvation

experience, but I certainly do have one to tell about my baptism.

Because both of my parents were fluent in Yoruba, the native language where they served as missionaries, my family attended a Yoruba-speaking church in one of the villages near our city. Our church did not have a baptistry, something that was true of most of the small village churches. Neither did we have an ordained pastor. Pastors in Nigeria were not automatically ordained just because they were pastors. Men wishing to be ordained had to pastor a church for a period of time, study Scripture, and go before a board who questioned them before they were granted the honor of being ordained. Hence, ordained pastors and churches with baptistries were a limited, if not rare, commodity where I lived. Consequently, the few larger churches with baptistries and ordained pastors would hold large baptisms a couple of times a year and baptize people from many smaller churches at the same time as a courtesy to those churches and pastors. (The Nigerian version of my denomination required that baptisms be done by someone who had been ordained. I realize that is not the case for all denominations worldwide.)

On the day of my baptism, I lined up behind a large number of people. I don't know how many there were altogether, but it must have been close to fifty. We all wore white robes and stood in single file spilling out the side door of the church into the sparse grass outside the church. I stood somewhere in the middle of the line, outside for a while, until one by one we made our way into the baptismal pool and out the other side door into the hot African sun to dry off. I was the only white person in that long line of people that day. It didn't feel at all unusual at the time. My family was the only white family in the church I attended, after all. My own pastor was a Nigerian, so it did not seem odd that a Nigerian pastor baptized me. Now, many years later, I treasure this fact. Most, if not all of the other American missionary kids attended the English-speaking church and if they were baptized while in Nigeria, it was done by one of their white missionary uncles. We had so many ordained pastors and theologians among our mission family that finding an American missionary to baptize a person was not hard.

Whether unique or ordinary, a baptism, demonstrating to others that a person has been saved, exemplifies God's goodness. God's very nature is good, and He cannot be anything other than good. He freely bestows His goodness on us in many ways, but the greatest of these is the gift of His Son Jesus, who died for our sins so that we might be saved. Psalm 31:19 says, "How abundant are the good things that you have stored up for those who fear you, that you bestow in the sight of all, on those who take refuge in you." The greatest of these good things is summed up in John 3:16, "For God so loved the world that he gave his one and only Son, that whoever believes in him shall not perish but have eternal life."

Prayer: Father, sometimes You give us extraordinary experiences in life, but of all the amazing gifts You have ever given, the gift of Jesus is the best. Thank You. In Jesus' name, Amen.

Thought for the Day: The greatest example of God's goodness is Jesus taking our sins upon Himself on the cross.

Day Four: Brighten the Corner Where You Are

By Shirley

Worship Hymn Focus

Brighten the Corner Where You Are

1913 by Ina D. Ogdon

God's goodness enables Christ-followers to receive salvation and experience His peace in the midst of anything that is happening in our lives. His Word says that "Every good and perfect gift is from above, coming down from the Father of the heavenly lights, who does not change like shifting shadows" (James 1:17).

How should we respond to the goodness of God? Our relationship with Him grows as He enables us to exhibit all the fruit of the Spirit while interacting with others. We learn to "Love [our] enemies, do good to those who hate [us], bless those who curse [us], pray for those who mistreat [us]" (Luke 6:27-28).

When we exhibit the fruit of goodness to others, through the goodness of God, we are able to lovingly interact with, teach, and admonish, thereby helping others to have a stronger relationship with God.

I have often heard people say that the Lord would provide a way for them to do certain great things they wanted to accomplish. Sadly, some people are so focused on finding that great thing that they miss many opportunities to serve the Lord by serving those who are right where they are, by doing what they may consider smaller things.

The energetic hymn, "Brighten the Corner Where You Are," written by Ina D. Ogdon reminds us to show goodness to people right where God places us.

My mom comes to mind as an example of someone who brightened the corner wherever she was. Since she had experienced the goodness of God, she was a shining light for Jesus, showing goodness to all those with whom she came in contact. As she showed goodness to others, she shared the Good News of Christ.

Stanza 1
Do not wait until some deed of greatness you may do,
Do not wait to shed your light afar;
To the many duties ever near you now be true,
Brighten the corner where you are.

Don't sit around waiting for a very important thing to do in a faraway place, look for opportunities to "let your light shine before others, that they may see your good deeds and glorify your Father in heaven" (Matthew 5:16). Show goodness to those around you right where God has placed you because "whoever can be trusted with very little can also be trusted with much" (Luke 16:10).

147

Refrain
Brighten the corner where you are!
Brighten the corner where you are!
Someone far from harbor you may guide across the bar;
Brighten the corner where you are!

Jesus said that as Christ-followers we are the light of the world (Matthew 5:14). He continued by reminding us not to "light a lamp and put it under a bowl" (Matthew 5:15), but instead to "let [our] light shine before others" (Matthew 5:16) so that those outside the harbor—a relationship with Christ—will be able to find their way over the sandbar and safely into the harbor.

Stanza 2
Just above are clouded skies that you may help to clear,
Let not narrow self your way debar;
Though into one heart alone may fall your song of cheer,
Brighten the corner where you are.

There are those around us who are in trouble, under clouded skies. We must not let our own self-interest stop us from showing goodness and looking out for the interests of others (Philippians 2:4). If we maintain our compassion for them, we may be able to help those around us bear their burdens. Even if our goodness helps only one person, we are to continue spreading goodness wherever we go, regardless of how few or many people we may help.

Stanza 3
Here for all your talent you may surely find a need,
Here reflect the bright and Morning Star;
Even from your humble hand the Bread of Life may feed,
Brighten the corner where you are.

God has equipped each Christ-follower with spiritual gifts and talents, as well as the fruit of the Spirit. We can look for opportunities to exercise those gifts and talents, and exhibit the fruit of the Spirit while we help meet those needs as we reflect Jesus, "the bright Morning Star" (Revelation 22:16). Our desire is to use our gifts, talents, and the fruit of the Spirit to offer the Bread of Life that comes from heaven, so that "whoever eats this bread will live forever" (John 6:48-51).

Prayer: Heavenly Father, thank You for Your goodness that enables us to receive salvation and experience Your peace. Give us eyes to recognize those around us who need to be shown goodness, so they can know You. In Jesus' name, Amen.

Thought for the Day: How are you showing goodness to others and brightening the corner where you are?

Day Five: God is Good All the Time

By Harriet

Today's Bible Nugget

In Luke 21:5-6 the disciples talk about the temple and how beautifully it was adorned. Then Jesus told them the days were coming when there would not be one stone left upon another. All would be torn down. This prophecy was literally fulfilled in AD 70 with the destruction of the temple. When the temple was set on fire, it blazed so hot all the gold that both adorned and was contained within the temple melted. The melted gold ran down in between the temple stones. Afterward, the Roman soldiers pulled the stones apart to retrieve the gold that was between them… until there was not one stone left upon another.

Where is God's goodness when bad things happen?

Crack! The crashing sound of thunder woke my friend and his wife from a sound sleep. Almost immediately they smelled smoke. They jumped out of bed and tried to turn a light on, only to find their house had no electricity. Fumbling around in the dark, my friend finally managed to find a flashlight and started walking around his dark house with his wife walking behind him. The smell of smoke grew stronger until it became apparent that their house had caught fire. He picked up the phone receiver from where it rested on the kitchen wall and dialed 911. Then the two ran out into their front yard in their pajamas and waited for help to arrive. Their house burned nearly to the ground that night from a fire caused by a direct lightning strike. Thanks to insurance they were able to rebuild, but they lost everything that was in their house that night.

Where is God's goodness when things like this happen?

I have always loved today's Bible nugget. I learned it in a Bible study many years ago and was struck then as I am still today with how wonderful it is when prophecy is so obviously and literally fulfilled. Today, this bit of information is amazing, but in AD 70 when the temple was being destroyed, the people felt devastation—not wonder or amazement.

That old expression that I've mentioned before comes to mind, "God is good all the time and all the time God is good." It's a true statement, though there are times when things certainly do not feel that way. I wish I could assure people that the awful, difficult, and sometimes even tragic things they experience somehow all make sense, but I can't... at least not in this life. There are things we go through in this life that we may never understand until we get to heaven, but that does not negate the truth of the old saying that God is good. He is, even in tough times.

God promises good to those of us who belong to Him, but His ways are not our ways and sometimes the way He works His good looks different than we might expect. My daughter, Kristin, wrote it this way in a paper she had to write for a class when she was attending a Christian college: "God's definition of good is different than man's definition. Man defines good as that which brings him a comfort of this life. God defines good as that which brings us closer to Him and is most glorifying to Him. God focuses on the eternal."

I have had some tough times in my life, some of which I write openly about. Others are more private and are known only to a few close friends and family members. During one of these times, I remember resigning myself to the fact that I might not ever understand why God had allowed certain things to happen, but that He must have had His reasons. In my prayer group, among people who knew my struggles, I would sometimes say, "Well, God does things for His glory." Every time I said this one of my friends would add, "And our good." It happened so many times that she drove the point home to my heart. She was correct—God does things for His glory and our good. He is good all the time, as the saying goes, even at a time when we might not feel like we can see His goodness.

Prayer: Heavenly Father, sometimes Your goodness to us is palpable, but sometimes we have to hold on to that truth in faith. Draw near to us when we are struggling or suffering. Help us to see Your goodness even when the circumstances we find ourselves in are not good from our perspective. In Jesus' name. Amen.

Thought for the Day: God's goodness is a truth that does not change according to our ability to see or understand it.

Week Seven:

Self-Control

Nuggets of Wonder from the New Testament Book of History

In the New Testament there is only one book in the "History" category, and it is the book of Acts. The history in Acts is that of the early church. The gospels do contain history also, in that they tell of Jesus and events during his time on earth, but the term "Book of History" in regard to the New Testament is primarily defined as the history of the early church, which can be found mostly in Acts. Though the author of this book does not name himself, evidence outside the scriptures and inferences from the book itself lead to the conclusion that Luke authored the book of Acts.[11]

Fruit of the Spirit, Self-Control

This week the focus is on the fruit of the Spirit, self-control. The Greek word *egkrateia* means mastery over oneself. This self-control comes through the power and

---

[11] Book of Acts - Read, Study Bible Verses Online (biblestudytools.com) accessed 8/3/22

Full url: https://www.biblestudytools.com/acts/ accessed 8/3/22

guidance of the Holy Spirit who gives us the ability to take control of our desires, thoughts, and actions.

"So I say, walk by the Spirit, and you will not gratify the desires of the flesh" (Galatians 5:16).

Day One: The Elephant Man

By Harriet

Today's Bible Nugget

Faith and repentance are two sides of the same coin. They are the flip sides of each other. Repentance is turning away from sin and faith is turning toward Christ. There is no true faith without a turning away from sin and there is no true repentance without a turning toward Christ. In the New Testament whenever the term faith is used, repentance is assumed, and when repentance is used, faith is assumed. An example of this can be seen in Acts 20:21, "I testified to both Jews and Greeks about repentance toward God and faith in our Lord Jesus" (CSB).

I called him "The Elephant Man," but his real name was David. He didn't speak much English, so whenever I bought an orange soft drink or snack from him, I'd just smile and hold out money for him to take. The man had only one leg, but he somehow managed to bring his container of snacks and soft drinks and a stool to the front of the mission hospital every day and sell his wares. He had steep competition for my weekly allowance of one shilling though, from the woman who sold British peppermints and the woman who sold freshly roasted peanuts, which we called groundnuts. Usually, the peppermints won out, but even those days, I'd pass him, and smile and he'd smile back.

Before I knew him, he had had two good legs, but while hunting for food one day he and a friend came upon an elephant and a fight with the animal ensued. I heard his story as a child, but my memory of it was greatly refreshed a few years ago when I had the blessing of reading about it. In the piece I read, missionary Melvin Wasson described the events of that fateful day and the days that followed, saying that one of the two hunters shot the elephant and then the men ran in opposite directions. The elephant didn't die; he charged at David instead. David managed to grab the elephant's tusk and avoided being gouged in the chest, but in the wrangling that ensued, the elephant ripped off a large part of David's leg. His friend soon reappeared and shot the elephant again, killing it. Then the friend went off to get help.

David worshiped the god "Ogun"—the Yoruba god of iron. David lay on the ground bleeding and fighting flies and ants off his wounded leg, fully believing that Ogun was thirsty for blood and was thus taking his life. Instead of David dying, his friend eventually returned with help. The two men carried David to the mission hospital where my parents worked and where missionary Melvin Wasson, who recorded this story in his personal notes, worked as the pharmacist. The doctors fought hard to save David's life and had to amputate his leg to do it. But he'd lost a lot of blood and needed a transfusion. This mission hospital, in the heart of Africa in the 1960s, did not have a well-stocked blood bank, so whenever the need arose for blood, they depended on volunteers. When David's family heard that he was considering getting a stranger's blood in his veins, they told him it would anger Ogun even more, and Ogun was already angry because David had lived. But the doctors informed him his best chance to live, and perhaps his only chance, was to accept the blood donations.

After a great internal struggle, David took the blood. Later, as he was recovering, he heard about Jesus who had shed His blood for him. David turned from his belief in Ogun, repented of his belief in a false god and accepted Christ as his Savior through faith.

Do you see the way repentance and faith work? When a person turns away from one thing, he is always turning toward another.

The Fruit of the Spirit we are focusing on this week is self-control. It is part of the repentance/faith picture, too, because lack of self-control results in all sorts of sins and evils that a person must then repent of and turn away from. Proverbs 25:28 warns that "Like a city whose walls are broken through is a person who lacks self-control." Sometimes it is only by faith and turning toward God for help that we can attain this self-control. Take finances, for example; it is much easier to spend our money on a plethora of things rather than tithing. We must repent of relying on our own judgment and accept in faith that obeying God is the right thing to do and then act with self-control to follow through. David had to repent of his belief in a false God, act with self-control to do the right thing against his family's warnings, and then turn in faith to do that right thing. Our circumstance may be different from David's but the steps we must go through are the same.

Prayer: Heavenly Father, grant us self-control where we have none. Help us to turn away from the things we should not be involved in and toward a closer walk with You. In Jesus' name, Amen.

Thought for the Day: Are your city walls, as referred to in the Proverbs verse, broken through? In what area of life do you need to increase your self-control?

Day Two: I Am Resolved

By Shirley

Worship Hymn Focus
I Am Resolved
1896 by Palmer Hartsough

Gaining an understanding of self-control through our understanding of God's character and commands gives us a better understanding of how to cultivate and exhibit the fruit of self-control in our own lives.

Let's remember David, the Elephant Man, who was mauled by an elephant, resulting in serious injuries. He lost so much blood that he required transfusions as part of his medical care at the mission hospital. During his recovery, David heard the Good News, repented of his sin, and through faith accepted Christ as his Savior. Harriet reminded us that repentance and faith work together so that when a person turns away from one thing, he is turning toward something else.

As Christ-followers we exercise self-control through our relationship with God as we grow in our understanding of Him and His Word. We learn to lean on Him for the power, strength, and enablement of the Holy Spirit to reign in our desires and actions so that we are thinking, saying, and doing things that glorify God (John 14:26).

Implied with self-control is the internal struggle between

our sinful desires we should control, not satisfy, and our desire to honor Christ in all that we think, say, and do. Our model for how to exhibit self-control is Jesus, who "for the joy set before him he endured the cross, scorning its shame, and sat down at the right hand of the throne of God" (Hebrews 12:2b).

What's important for Christ-followers is that God is glorified when we exercise self-control. "Strenuously contend with all the energy Christ so powerfully works in [us]" (Colossians 1:29) so that we know how "to live self-controlled, upright and godly lives in this present age" (Titus 2:12b).

Palmer Hartsough wrote the lyrics of the magnificent hymn "I Am Resolved." As we sing this hymn, we express our resolve, or determination (employ self-control) as we go to Jesus who has "the words of eternal life" (John 6:68).

Stanza 1
I am resolved no longer to linger,
Charmed by the world's delight,
Things that are higher, things that are nobler,
These have allured my sight.

Here we resolve not to continue being tempted to sin by the world's delights. Instead, since we are Christ-followers, we will "set [our] hearts on things above, where Christ is, seated at the right hand of God. Set [our] minds on things above, not on earthly things" (Colossians 3:1-2).

Refrain
I will hasten to Him,
Hasten so glad and free;
Jesus, greatest, highest,
I will come to Thee.

We resolve to come to Jesus for salvation if we are not saved, and for forgiveness of our unconfessed sin if we are saved. As Christ-followers we resolve not to hesitate to come to Jesus for help, comfort, and communion.

Stanza 2
I am resolved to go to the Savior,
Leaving my sin and strife,
He is the true One, He is the Just One
He hath the words of life.

Resolve to go to the Savior, Jesus Messiah, leave sin and strife behind, and come to Him for salvation. By faith we know that He is the true and just God who has the "words of life."

Stanza 3
I am resolved to follow the Savior,
Faithful and true each day,
Heed what He sayeth, do what He willeth,
He is the living way.

Here we resolve to follow the Savior. Once we become Christ-followers, we must obey and follow Him as Lord. We know what we should do because He left us the Holy Spirit-inspired Bible to teach us about who God is and what He requires of us.

Stanza 4

I am resolved to enter the kingdom,
Leaving the paths of sin;
Friends may oppose me, foes may beset me,
Still will I enter in.

In this stanza the hymn writer expresses a resolve to enter God's kingdom on earth, leaving everything behind, so we "will know how people ought to conduct themselves in God's household, which is the church of the living God, the pillar and foundation of the truth" (1 Timothy 3:15).

Stanza 5

I am resolved, and who will go with me?
Come, friends, without delay;
Taught by the Bible, led by the Spirit,
We'll walk the heavenly way.

Finally, there is a resolve to share the Good News with all those whom the Lord brings across our paths and ask them to come follow Christ with us. Because we are taught by the Bible and led by the Holy Spirit, we must walk alongside others in disciple-making relationships helping them to understand how to follow Christ.

Prayer: Heavenly Father, thank You for Your Holy Spirit who enables us to exercise self-control. In Jesus' name, Amen.

Thought for the Day: In what areas of your life do you need resolve to exercise self-control?

Day Three: Are You Sleeping?

By Harriet

Today's Bible Nugget

Acts 20:8-10 tells an interesting story. One night while the apostle Paul was preaching a really long sermon, a man resting on a windowsill dozed off, fell out the window, and was presumed dead. Paul ran down and threw himself on the man and then announced that the man was not dead after all. Was the man actually dead and brought back to life by Paul or just knocked unconscious from the fall and then revived by Paul? I do not know, and it doesn't seem to me that the Bible is completely clear on it either. I've always found this an interesting story. For those of us who sometimes find ourselves trying not to go to sleep during church, it's comforting to know we aren't the first to have this problem. And for my preacher friends, don't feel bad, they fell asleep when Paul was preaching too.

This lesser-known passage first came to my attention many years ago, early in my writing career. Along with being an author and freelance writer, I also substitute teach at a Christian school and one day at work, I shared with a fellow teacher the fact that I was beginning to write. In explaining this I made the comment that writing felt more fluid to me than even speaking and I thought I wrote better than I spoke.

I said, "You know, I think maybe the apostle Paul was like that. He isn't known for his sermons and orations as much as for his writings."

My friend's response made me burst out laughing. He said, "Absolutely. I think so too. After all, his preaching was so non-notable that a man fell asleep during a sermon, fell out a window, and nearly died!"

Maybe Paul was a better writer than speaker, and maybe as the passage says, "the hour was late" and Paul was talking "on and on." Still, falling asleep while sitting on a windowsill is the man's own fault. A little self-control might have come in handy for this poor man. This seems to me to have been a nearly lethal case of lack of self-control.

The inability to stay awake is seen at another spot in the New Testament when the disciples could not stay awake. Matthew 26:36-46 tells the story of Jesus praying the garden of Gethsemane before His betrayal, trial, and eventual crucifixion. He took Peter, James, and John with Him and told them to pray while He went off to pray alone. Jesus came back and found them asleep. In verses 40-41 "'Couldn't you men keep watch with me for one hour?' he asked Peter. 'Watch and pray so that you will not fall into temptation. The spirit is willing, but the flesh is weak.'"

Sadly, this scene is repeated again and again. Three times Jesus asks the disciples to stay awake and pray and three times they fail to do so and fall asleep. Have you ever missed something important because you fell asleep? I sometimes watch television while in my bed at night. More times than I'd like to admit, I have missed something important in a movie I was watching or the end of a ball game because I dozed off. These examples pale in comparison to the disciples falling asleep instead of praying just before the greatest moment in all history—both earthly and eternal.

Yet Jesus in His mercy loved them anyway, even with their shortcomings. He gives acknowledgment to the fact that their bodies were tired when He said, "…the flesh is weak." There's an Old Testament verse that shows God understands, too. We see it in Psalm 78:39 which says, "He remembered that they were but flesh, a passing breeze that does not return."

We too have flesh that is weak. We too are just human beings with all our weaknesses. It's comforting to know that God understands, but nonetheless, working to increase our self-control in all areas is a noble goal.

Prayer: Heavenly Father, You are so gracious to us, extending us mercy when we fall short as we do so often in so many ways. Thank You Lord for loving us just the way we are, but also thank You for being in the business of growing us into better people. Increase our self-control and use us for Your glory. In Jesus' name, Amen.

Thought for the Day: Are you sleeping in your efforts to gain better self-control in some aspect of your life? Wake up. Get to work.

Day Four: Be Still, My Soul

By Shirley

Worship Hymn Focus
Be Still, My Soul
1752 by Katharina A. von Schlegel

We have looked at exercising self-control by choosing to think, speak, and act in order to honor God. As we strive to remain faithful to God and follow His commands, sometimes everything around us continues to be chaotic, and even gets worse. We do our best to remain faithful to God and follow His commands, yet it is at these times that we can be caught off guard and begin doubting God.

Let's dig a little deeper and look at a beautiful hymn, "Be Still, My Soul," for which Katharina A. von Schlegel wrote the lyrics. This hymn reminds us to be still and trust God—to exercise self-control—in the midst of any situation.

Romans 12:2 tells us to "be transformed by the renewing of [our] mind." As we remind ourselves to be still and trust in God, we are renewing our minds through His Word.

Stanza 1
Be still, my soul: the Lord is on thy side.
Bear patiently the cross of grief or pain.
Leave to thy God to order and provide;
In every change, He faithful will remain.
Be still, my soul: thy best, thy heav'nly Friend
Through thorny ways leads to a joyful end.

Since the Lord is on our side—actually, we are on His side—we can patiently bear whatever grief or pain comes our way. We remind ourselves that we can trust God to order our steps and provide for our needs because He will always be faithful. Knowing the Lord is faithful helps us exercise self-control and patience while He fulfills His promise that leads us to our joyful end.

Stanza 2
Be still, my soul: thy God doth undertake
To guide the future, as He has the past.
Thy hope, thy confidence let nothing shake;
All now mysterious shall be bright at last.
Be still, my soul: the waves and winds still know
His voice who ruled them while He dwelt below.

It is God who guides our circumstances (past, present, and future). We can trust Him and not worry about what may happen to us. We see His power to lead and protect us in His rule over the wind and waves.

Stanza 3
Be still, my soul: when dearest friends depart,
And all is darkened in the vale of tears,
Then shalt thou better know His love, His heart,
Who comes to soothe thy sorrow and thy fears.
Be still, my soul: thy Jesus can repay.
From His own fullness all He takes away.

We can be still because God comforts us when we face

the death of dear family and friends by soothing our grieving hearts and dispersing our fears.

Stanza 4

Be still, my soul: the hour is hast'ning on
When we shall be forever with the Lord.
When disappointment, grief, and fear are gone,
Sorrow forgot, love's purest joys restored.
Be still, my soul: when change and tears are past
All safe and blessed we shall meet at last.

The time when we will be with the Lord is coming soon. Since we trust the Lord, we are able to anticipate the time when disappointment, grief, and fear are gone, and we will forget our sorrow as we eagerly await meeting Him (1 Thessalonians 4:16-18). What a wonderful truth that allows us to remain still and not be anxious!

Stanza 5

Be still, my soul: begin the song of praise
On earth, believing, to Thy Lord on high;
Acknowledge Him in all thy words and ways,
So shall He view thee with a well-pleased eye.
Be still, my soul: the Sun of life divine
Through passing clouds shall but more brightly shine.

Our soul is stilled while we are here on earth as we sing praises to the Lord in heaven. We please Him by acknowledging Him in all we say and do (Proverbs 3:5-7). God's faithfulness will lead us to spend eternity in heaven.

Prayer: Heavenly Father, thank You that in the midst of anything that happens in our lives, we can be still and trust that You are with us, guiding, comforting, and preserving us. In Jesus' name, Amen.

Thought for the Day: What things in your life do you need to leave in God's hands to order your steps and provide for your needs?

Day Five: Running Aground

By Harriet

Today's Bible Nugget

Sometimes verses strike me as humorous. This one did just that when I read it with fresh eyes one day. Just before Paul's shipwreck, he had a dream in which God told him he would appear before Caesar. Afterward Paul tells the men on his ship, "Keep up your courage men, for I believe God that it will turn out exactly as I have been told. But we must run aground on some island" (Acts 27:25-26). Maybe there's something wrong or irreverent about me for finding these verses hilarious. Or maybe I've just been there too many times in my life. But I can truly relate to these words, "Things are going to be okay. I believe God! Um... but first we are going to have a major shipwreck. There will be pieces of us everywhere—a major mess! Just overlook it. Everything is going to turn out exactly the way God wants it to!

We've all experienced times in our lives when even with all the self-control we can muster, tough things still come our way. Bad things just happen sometimes, even to good people. The rain falls on the just and the unjust, as Matthew 5:45 reminds us.

Remember the friend I wrote about in a prior devotion whose house caught on fire? Neither he nor his wife did anything wrong. Their house was clean and well cared for. They did not act carelessly with electronics, matches, or any other fire-starter or hazard. They even had a fire alarm in their house with working batteries. Yet, as they slept soundly in their beds, a bolt of lightning shot down from the sky, hitting the roof of their house and instantly setting it on fire. Their home burned to the ground that night. They lost everything they owned except for their lives.

February 5, 2008, one of my sons called me from college saying, "Mom, pray, we've just been hit by a tornado. Gotta go." I told my husband, who was working at his desk in his home office, on my way up to my room to pray as my son had asked. My husband confessed later that he didn't actually pray because he figured if our son had called then he was okay, it sounded like the danger was past, and he added, "You know how kids tend to exaggerate."

My son's plea for prayers was no exaggeration. He was a senior at Union University in Jackson, Tennessee, that day when it was hit by a devasting EF-4 tornado. He told us later that they heard an announcement on their suite intercom to immediately seek shelter because a tornado was approaching. He and his suitemates piled into their common inner bathroom and closed the door, but outside the door he could hear what sounded like a freight train. After the sound ended, they opened the door to see what was left of their living room area. They made their way out their front door, but because my son was barefoot, he went into his room to get shoes. As he was retrieving his shoes his front door caved in. He was still able to escape the building through his blown-out bedroom window. The school directed the students to a central building that had less damage. That's where he called me from, but as it turned out he couldn't talk long because he quickly started helping assess the damage and freeing others who were trapped. Though there were some injuries and the school sustained forty million dollars' worth of damage, miraculously, no one died.

This tornado didn't happen because of someone's carelessness. It just happened.

I've had challenges and painful chapters in my life, finding myself in circumstances over which I had no control. Some of these, I sometimes talk about in my writings, but others are too personal. Through them I have learned an important lesson: there is a God, and I'm not Him.

Ever since I read this verse that day that it struck me funny, when unforeseen things happen, I find myself shaking my head and saying, "I've run aground on that island again."

Prayer: Heavenly Father, ultimately You are the one who controls the things in my world. Keep me mindful of that truth and submissive to Your will. In Jesus' name, Amen.

Thought for the Day: It's good to increase your self-control but give yourself some grace when you find you've run aground. Sometimes unwelcome things happen that are simply out of our control.

Week Eight:

Love

Nuggets of Wonder from the Pauline Epistles

The Pauline Epistles were letters written to the early Church by the apostle, Paul. He wrote more books of the Bible than any other author—including Moses, Solomon, and any of the original apostles. Paul's ancient epistles contain valuable insight into modern-day Christian living, while also providing a snapshot of the early Christian Church.[12] There are thirteen books included in the Pauline Epistles, but some think the book of Hebrews was also written by Paul which, if included, would make fourteen. In this devotional book we have placed Hebrews in the General Epistles category since its authorship is not known.

The thirteen Pauline Epistle books are: Romans, 1 & 2 Corinthians, Galatians, Ephesians, Philippians, Colossians, 1 & 2 Thessalonians, 1 & 2 Timothy, Titus, and Philemon.

Fruit of the Spirit, Love

This week the focus is on the fruit of the Spirit, love. The

---

[12] What Are the Pauline Epistles? (lifehopeandtruth.com) accessed 8/3/22

Greek word *agape* means selfless love, choosing to put other people before ourselves, and sacrificing ourselves for their benefit. Love is not merely a sentimental emotion.

"As the Father has loved me, so have I loved you. Now remain in my love. If you keep my commands, you will remain in my love, just as I have kept my Father's commands and remain in his love. I have told you this so that my joy may be in you and that your joy may be complete" (John 15:9-11).

Day One: A Love Story

By Harriet

Today's Bible Nugget

God created the world by speaking words. He said, "Let there be light" and there was light, "Let the earth sprout vegetation" and it did, and so forth. We can read about it in the creation story found in Genesis 1. Interestingly, that is what happens again when we speak God's Word to unbelievers; God again brings about a new creation by His Word. As 2 Corinthians 5:17 tells us, "Therefore, if any man is in Christ, he is a new creature; the old things have passed away; behold new things have come" (NASB). Ah! The power of a word!

Johannes Gutenberg, Thomas Edison, Betsy Ross, and George Washington Carver. What do these people have in common? They are all creators. Johannes Gutenberg invented the printing press, Thomas Edison invented the electric light bulb, Betsy Ross created the first American flag, and George Washington Carver came up with three hundred different uses for peanuts. I could go on and on listing people and the creations they came up with without which our world today would be quite different. There are inventors of small things, too, that changed our world, like Velcro, for instance, which was invented by a man names George de Mestral, or Sticky

Notes, invented in 1968 by a man named Spencer Silver, or Liquid Paper, invented by Bette Nesmith Graham who happened to be the mother of Mike Nesmith. Mike is best known as one of the musically talented actors who achieved fame as a member of the sixties pop group, "The Monkees." Little known fact—Mike Nesmith was the wealthiest of all the Monkees band members, not because of his musical ability but because of his inheritance from his mother's Liquid Paper patent and royalties.

The number of people throughout history who have created something, big or small, that has profoundly impacted our world would be so long that it would be almost impossible to compile. People are creators by nature. Even those of us who never create or invent anything earth-shattering that might forever impact the world still create things in our own home and lives every day. Maybe it's a new way to do something that works better than the old, a new design for an old room, or a new baked item fresh from the oven that is making the whole house smell yummy. We love to create.

We were made in God's image and because of that truth there are many things we do that reflect God. Being creative and naturally creating new things is one of the ways we reflect God and demonstrate our likeness to Him. God created the world and everything in it according to Acts 17:24, so our inclination to create is just us scratching that creative itch God placed in us. He graciously gives us dominions of our own in which to create, but sometimes God also lets us join Him in creating something eternal. Scripture tells us in 2 Corinthians that He makes a new creature by washing a person's sins away and saving this person's soul. This happens when they accept Jesus as their Savior. One of the most common ways that happens is when you or I share the gospel with someone.

When we share the story of Jesus' death and resurrection with an unbeliever, we are sharing the story of God's love. John 3:16, "For God so loved the world that he gave his only begotten son...." This is the gospel message. It is a message of love—the greatest of all loves. In John 15:13, Jesus said, "Greater love has no one than this: to lay down one's life for one's friends." That is exactly what Jesus did. He laid down his life for sinners like you and me so that we could be forgiven of our sins and gain eternal life. And in doing this, we become new creatures too. What a marvelous love story is ours in this story of a Savior who loved us enough to die for us. How can we help but share it?

Prayer: Heavenly Father, the story of Your love for us is the greatest love story of all time. And it's a story we have the privilege of sharing with others who desperately need to hear it. When we do, we are contributing to Your creative work as You make new creations of those who accept Your gift of salvation. What an amazing privilege is ours. Thank You. In Jesus' name, Amen.

Thought for the Day: We are the beneficiaries of such a great love story, and we get to participate in God's creative work when we share this story with others.

Day Two: O Love That Will Not Let Me Go

By Shirley

Worship Hymn Focus
O Love That Will Not Let Me Go
1882 by George Matheson

The more we experience and understand the depth of God's love, the more we gain a fuller understanding of how to cultivate and exhibit the fruit of love in our own lives.

God is love (1 John 4:8); He is the source of love (1 John 4:7-12); and He chooses to direct His love toward us (Ephesians 2:4-5). We know that "God so loved the world that he gave his one and only Son, that whoever believes in him shall not perish but have eternal life" (John 3:16). The Bible tells us that Jesus laid down His life for sinners like us so we can be forgiven our sins and have eternal life. God's love heals, protects, and overcomes (1 Corinthians 13).

God loves His people with a love that is all-powerful, all-knowing, and ever-present. This love does not always spare us from tragedies or illnesses. When our circumstances appear hopeless, God is faithful. His love gives us the strength we need to walk through anything we may encounter.

God's love heals our souls when we put our faith and trust in Him as Savior and Lord (Hebrews 11:6). His love also heals so much more. God's love heals our emotional wounds, our relationships, and our calloused and hardened hearts, just to name a few.

God's love protects us in ways that are not always how we want or expect to be protected. As we love others, we do everything we can to protect them from spiritual, emotional, mental, and physical things that can do them harm.

God's love overcomes. It overcomes sin and fear, and because of God's love we can overcome anything that may come against us. God's love is all-powerful and all-conquering.

A splendid hymn, "O Love That Will Not Let Me Go," written by George Matheson, reminds us that God loves us "with an everlasting love" (Jeremiah 31:3).

Stanza 1

O Love that will not let me go,
I rest my weary soul in thee;
I give thee back the life I owe,
That in thine ocean depths its flow
May richer, fuller be.

We can be assured of God's love because "neither death nor life, neither angels nor demons, neither the present nor the future, nor any powers, neither height nor depth, nor anything else in all creation, will be able to separate us from the love of God that is in Christ Jesus our Lord" (Romans 8:38-39). Jesus invites us to come to Him for rest when we are weary (Matthew 11:28-29). Because of God's love we can have communion and fellowship with Him.

Stanza 2
O Light that foll'west all my way,
I yield my flick'ring torch to thee;
My heart restores its borrowed ray,
That in thy sunshine's blaze its day
May brighter, fairer be.

Jesus said, "I am the light of the world. Whoever follows me will not walk in darkness but will have the light of life" (John 8:12). I give Him my torch with its unsteady flame so that the Light of Christ can restore our light. Through His Word, God makes the sunshine blaze so we can clearly see the path we are to walk.

Stanza 3
O Joy that seekest me through pain,
I cannot close my heart to thee;
I trace the rainbow through the rain,
And feel the promise is not vain,
That morn shall tearless be.

God, here referred to as Joy, seeks and directs us to receive salvation from our sin. The Joy is described as the rainbow, God's symbol of promise that He would never destroy the world by flood again (Genesis 9:13-15). The original lyrics were "I climb the rainbow through the rain." My recollection is that a hymnal committee of the Church of Scotland insisted Matheson change "climb" to "trace." There is a huge difference between standing inside, sheltered from the rain and tracing a rainbow on the inside windowsill, versus actually being out in the rain and climbing that rainbow, isn't there?

Stanza 4
O Cross that liftest up my head,
I dare not ask to fly from thee;
I lay in dust life's glory dead,
And from the ground there blossoms red
Life that shall endless be.

The Cross represents salvation. Because of the finished work of Jesus Christ on the cross, we can lift our heads knowing that God is our deliverer (Psalm 3:3). Therefore, we will not seek to escape, we will glory in it (Galatians 6:14). The red symbolizes the shed blood of Jesus who was "an atoning sacrifice for our sins" (1 John 4:10).

Prayer: Heavenly Father, thank You for Your all-powerful, all-knowing, and ever-present love which gives us salvation, sanctifies us, and will glorify us in heaven. In Jesus' name, Amen.

Thought for the Day: God's love heals, protects, and overcomes.

Day Three: Loving all People

By Harriet

Today's Bible Nugget

Zechariah 8:4-5 says, "Thus says the Lord of hosts, 'Old men and old women will again sit in the streets of Jerusalem, each man with his staff in his hand because of age. And the streets of the city will be filled with boys and girls playing in the streets.'"

When I studied Zechariah in an inductive Bible study, my teacher quoted a man by the name of Speers whom she found in her Expository Bible Commentary as saying, "Too often men measure a city's significance by its business, professions, industry, its buildings, its wealth, its art and culture. Zechariah suggests we measure the significance of our cities by their effect upon two groups easily overlooked—the old and the young."

Why does this nugget from Zechariah appear in the section under Pauline Epistles? The answer is simple—Paul writes about treating all people with love—all people—the young, old, even the poor and downtrodden. In Galatians 2:10, for instance, Paul writes, "All they asked was that we remember the poor, the very thing I had been eager to do all along."

Paul was a man of the law. He was educated in it,

practiced it, and valued it so much that until his life-changing encounter with Jesus on the road to Damascus, he persecuted people, especially Christians who he felt did not adhere to the law as he understood it. How did a man like that—a man who at least stood nearby and probably participated in the stoning of Stephen, the first Christian martyr—become a man who learned to love others so much that he risked his life sharing the gospel to the Gentiles? He also spoke, wrote, and taught the importance of love. There are many answers to this question. As we read about in a previous devotion, becoming a follower of Jesus Christ makes a person a new creature, and this truth can definitely be seen in Paul's life. But also, in keeping with Paul's love of the law, one certain reason he changed so completely was his new understanding of the true meaning of what keeping the law was all about. He summed it up in Romans 13:8 where he wrote: "Let no debt remain outstanding, except the continuing debt to love one another, for whoever loves others has fulfilled the law."

My mother was a magnet for the downtrodden. My dad used to tease that my mom wore a sign on her back she didn't know she wore that said, "Hi. I'm Alice. Please tell me your problems." Consequently, one of the greatest lessons I ever learned from my mother was to never judge another person by outward things such as looks, status, money, etc. Perhaps the reason my mom knew this so well traced back to her childhood.

Mom was born the third child of a poor, mostly

uneducated farmer. My grandfather had only a third-grade education before he had to drop out of school to work in the nearby textile mills to help his family. As a grown man, he continued to work in those mills as he also worked his farm while supporting four children, a wife, and his wife's unmarried sister.

My mom met my dad when she was in nursing school, and he was a medical student. My dad was also the son and grandson of doctors. When he was coming home to meet her family my grandfather was beside himself with worry about what would happen when this "young doctor," as Granddaddy called him, saw the rural farm and the small house he had built by hand. This four-room wooden house had no running water or indoor plumbing—they drew their water from a well and used an outhouse instead. Granddaddy told Mom, "That young doctor is going to take one look at this place, leave, and never come back." Mom being the person she always was, replied. "If he does, then he's not the man I want anyway." He didn't. My dad loved Mom even more for her hard-working, but low socio-economic position in society. They married and shared sixty-three years and a whole lot of children and grandchildren before God took her unexpectedly when she was eighty-six. My mother loved the downtrodden because she had been one of them herself, so she understood their plight.

Paul loved the downtrodden for a different reason. When God saved him, He miraculously filled Paul's heart with love for others and his head with an understanding that love is what God is all about. Paul, a man who loved the law, came to realize that love is the law. It's God's law.

Prayer: Heavenly Father, fill our hearts with love, too. Open our eyes to see needs around us and give us the grace to extend ourselves wherever we can to help those in need. In Jesus' name, Amen.

Thought for the Day: The downtrodden are all around us. There but for the grace of God go we.

Day Four: Make Me a Channel of Blessing

By Shirley

Worship Hymn Focus
Make Me a Channel of Blessing
1903 by Harper G. Smith

As we continue looking at love as a fruit of the Spirit, let's dig a little deeper. In 1 John 4:11-12, we read that "since God so loved us, we also ought to love one another. No one has ever seen God; but if we love one another, God lives in us, and his love is made complete in us." We demonstrate our love for God by loving others.

Harper G. Smith wrote the challenging hymn, "Make Me a Channel of Blessing." Through the lyrics of this hymn, Christ-followers are challenged to love and serve others. We are told how we can be channels of blessing for God through the prophet Zechariah (8:13b) who wrote "[God] will save you, and you will be a blessing." When we have received and experienced the love of God and His salvation, we cannot help but share this love with those around us.

Refrain
Make me a channel of blessing today,
Make me a channel of blessing, I pray;
My life possessing, my service blessing,
Make me a channel of blessing today.

The refrain is a prayer that God would make us channels of blessing to those whom He brings across our paths. This means God uses us as instruments through which His blessings flow to others. We continue praying that He would possess our lives and bless our service to Him. Paul David Tripp gives a little more insight when he says, "when God calls me to Himself, He also calls me to be a servant, an instrument in His redeeming hands."[13] We allow God's love to flow through us to others as we tell them what Jesus did for us with His gift of salvation.

Stanza 1
Is your life a channel of blessing?
Is the love of God flowing through you?
Are you telling the lost of the Savior?
Are you ready His service to do?

How well are we, as Christ-followers, following God's command to "bring salvation to the ends of the earth" by showing the light of God to the dark, lost world (Acts 13:47)? We are to serve God, letting His light shine in and through us to those who are weary and heavy laden.

Stanza 2
Is your life a channel of blessing?
Are you burdened for those who are lost?
Have you urged upon those who are straying

---

[13] Paul David Trip, Instruments in the Redeemer's Hands (Phillipsburg, NJ: P&R Publishing, 2002), xi.

The Savior who died on the cross?

Singing this stanza helps us examine whether or not we are following God's commands. Do we have a burden for the lost and a desire to see them saved? Are we telling those who don't know God or are straying from Him how they can be reconciled to Him (2 Corinthians 5:18-20)? Our recognition of what Christ did for us on the cross grows a burden for the lost to be reconciled to God through Jesus Christ.

Stanza 3
Is your life a channel of blessing?
Is it daily telling for Him?
Have you spoken the Word of salvation
To those who are dying in sin?

This stanza provides another opportunity for us to examine whether we are following God's commands. Is talking with and telling others about Jesus a natural and regular part of our encounters with people? Are we simply inviting people to church, or are we sharing the gospel with them? The last line provides our impetus for telling others about Jesus. We are to share the gospel of Jesus Christ with all those with whom we come in contact because the world is filled with people who are dying in their sin and need to know how to be saved.

Stanza 4
We cannot be channels of blessing
If our lives are not free from known sin;
We will barriers be and a hindrance
To those we are trying to win.

This stanza reminds us that we cannot continue living with known and unconfessed sin in our lives. If we continue to sin, we will become barriers and hindrances to those with whom we are sharing the gospel. When the Holy Spirit convicts us of sin, we need to be quick to confess that sin, ask the Lord for forgiveness, and then walk in the freedom of that forgiveness.

Prayer: Heavenly Father, thank You for Your love that saved us and sustains us every moment of every day. Make me a channel of blessing through which Your love flows. In Jesus' name, Amen.

Thought for the Day: In what ways is your life a channel of blessing?

Day Five: The Truth about Love

By Harriet

Today's Bible Nugget

Isaiah 65:16 calls God the God of truth. But the Hebrew actually uses the word "amen" in the place of the word truth. What is meant by this? It is explained in 2 Corinthians 1:20 which says, "For all the promises of God find their Yes in him. That is why it is through Him that we utter our Amen to God for His glory" (ESV).

This word that we translate as "amen," is used mostly at the end of someone's writings or statements; for example, many of Paul's letters end this way, as does Revelation. Jesus, however, often said it at the beginning of His talks. It is often interpreted as "verily" but the Hebrew word Jesus spoke was "amen." He frequently began this way and sometimes Jesus even said it twice as he started speaking. Why? Because Jesus is truth!

The passage in today's nugget tells us that God is the God of truth, and that Jesus also is truth. Jesus actually said this in John 14:6 when He said he was "the way, the truth and the life." But do you know what else God is? Can you recall a verse you may have learned as a child that specifically says God is a certain thing? What is that thing? 1 John 4:8 is the verse I am thinking of. It says, "Whoever does not love does not know God, because God is love." And there it is—God is truth, and He is also love.

Hesed and *emet*. Do you know these words? I confess I didn't until I had the incredible blessing of sitting under the teaching of world-renowned Septuagint scholar, Dr. Peter Gentry, whom I quote often in this book. He joined my small inner-city church because his daughter had become good friends and eventual roommates with our pastor's daughter in college. Of course, our church utilized him quickly and made him the adult Sunday school teacher. Yes, "the" teacher—we only had one adult class because our church was so small.

You can't sit under this great man's teaching for as many years as I did without learning the terms *hesed* and *emet*. He even had the word *hesed* put on his car's license plate. If you are ever anywhere and see a car with a license plate that says "hesed," it's likely you have happened to be at the same place as Dr. Gentry, or his wife Barbara. This man, who read the Scripture to us during class straight from his Hebrew or Greek Bible, loved these two words.

What do they mean? They mean love and truth. *Hesed* means love and *emet* means truth. *Hesed* and *emet* are one of those word pairs that the Hebrews loved to use in their writings that show up so often in the Old Testament. Some examples of word pairs we see in the Old Testament are faith and repentance, like I wrote about in the Elephant Man devotion in an earlier chapter. Other examples include justice and righteousness, law and covenant, kindness and faithfulness, and love and truth—*hesed* and *emet*.

Hesed is such a rich term that translators have often found it hard to translate into English. In different versions of the Bible it is translated as love, loving-kindness, steadfast love, and mercy. One reason for this is that words in Hebrew are somewhat less static than their English translations. So, *hesed* is not just a thing—love—it is an action too. God's *hesed* for us is not just a fact; it is an ongoing, everyday action on His part. Likewise, *emet* is not just truth in the way English often defines the word. It is not just a fact, a static thing. *Emet* is an ongoing dynamic, much like when we say someone is our spouse, we aren't just stating a fact—we are revealing an ongoing special relationship we have with this person.

I'm not sure I have been able to offer adequate insights in this devotion about these two words, *hesed* and *emet*, or as the English call them, love and truth. Certainly, you who are reading this have not gained the kind of insight I did sitting under this brilliant scholar week after week for so many years. But hopefully, you have at least gotten an inkling about these treasured Hebrew words that reflect who God is more accurately than any other two words in all of the languages of all of time. Though they are Hebrew words and Paul wrote in Greek when he wrote his epistles, he wrote about the concepts—he wrote about love and truth.

Prayer: Loving Father, Your love for us and to us is ongoing. You are truth and everything we read about You in Your

Word is true. And in Your love, You teach us truth. Thank You. In Jesus' name, Amen.

Thought for the Day: Now you can add these two new wonderful words to your vocabulary—*hesed* and *emet.*

Week Nine:

Gentleness

Nuggets of Wonder from the General Epistles

The General Epistles are books composed of letters to the churches in general rather than to a specific church. There are seven books that are consistently considered a part of the General Epistles, but in this devotional, we have added Hebrews, making eight books in this category. The author of Hebrews is not known. Since Paul is suspected as a strong possibility, often Hebrews is included in the Pauline Epistles, but other times it is listed with the General Epistles as we have chosen to do.

The books in this category are: Hebrews, James, 1 & 2 Peter, 1, 2, & 3 John, and Jude.

Fruit of the Spirit, Gentleness

This week the focus is on the fruit of the Spirit, gentleness. The Greek word *prautes* does not have an exact English meaning. It is difficult to define because it refers to an inward attitude. It includes submission to God, humility to learn, and showing consideration for others. Contrary to what some believe, gentleness is not weakness. Gentleness encompasses courage, strength, and resolve to persevere.

"In your relationships with one another, have the same

mindset as Christ Jesus: Who, being in very nature God, did not consider equality with God something to be used to his own advantage; rather, he made himself nothing by taking the very nature of a servant, being made in human likeness" (Philippians 2:5-7).

Day One: Understanding the Book of Hebrews

By Harriet

Today is a little different. Hebrews is only one of the books in the General Epistles but through the years I managed to collect two nuggets related to it. So today, I will share two nuggets instead of only one.

Bible Nugget #1 about the Book of Hebrews

Who wrote the book of Hebrews? Truthfully, no one really knows for sure. The most common belief is that Paul wrote it. However, there are some significant differences in this book and Paul's other books. It doesn't start the same way, and the Old Testament quotes are from the Septuagint, whereas Paul usually quoted the original Hebrew. There are other differences, too. If not Paul, then who? Possible authors include Luke, Barnabas, Priscilla (the wife of Aquila), and Clement of Rome, as well as others. One real possibility is that it was one of Paul's sermons which was transcribed by someone else. But my father always claimed with a twinkle in his eye, and his tongue in his cheek, that he thought Priscilla was the author because in Hebrews 13:22, the writer says he has written in "few words" (KJV), and who but a woman could write thirteen chapters and call it "few words?"

Bible Nugget #2 about the Book of Hebrews

Hebrews is the "Better Than" book. This New Testament book points the way to a better life. In it you will find references to things that are better many, many times. It tells us that Christ is: better than angels (1:4), worthy of more glory than Moses (3:3), the builder of the house (the Creator) and as such has more honor than the creation (3:4), a great High Priest (4:14) that is better than man's high priests (5:1-2). Men swear by things that are better than themselves, but God swears by Himself (because He is better—6:13-16). Hebrews also tells of:

- a better covenant enacted on better promises (8:6),
- a greater, more perfect tabernacle (9:11),
- a better possession (10:34),
- a kingdom which cannot be shaken (a better kingdom—12:28),
- and a better city (11:10 and 13:14).

What could be better than this?

Along with my silly father's attempt at humor, these nuggets offer an overall glimpse of the book of Hebrews, but since this week's focus is on gentleness, we will derive today's devotion from Hebrews 5:1-9.

The first two verses in Hebrews 5 talk about human priests. In verse 2, in the context of human priests, the writer, whoever he or she was, wrote, "He is able to deal gently with those who are ignorant and are going astray, since he himself is subject to weakness."

Then in verses 5-10 the writer compares human priests with Christ. Unlike a human priest, Jesus was sinless, but He still knew temptation and underwent great suffering so He can deal gently with failures in His people because he knows what it is like to have been tempted and to suffer.

How much more gently should we deal with others in our everyday lives? The second year I was married, the house where we lived had deep ditches on both sides of our driveway at the point where the driveway fed into the street. These were drainage ditches that ran along the edge of the street for drainage in that spot of our subdivision. A pipe ran under our driveway at this point to connect the two ditches. One Saturday when my husband was home, as I backed my car out to make a run to the grocery store, I accidentally dropped one wheel into one of the ditches. I turned off my car, put it in park with that one wheel deep in the ditch, and went in to ask my husband for help. Up to this point in our relationship I had not done something this careless or potentially destructive and expensive, so I didn't know how he would respond to my poor driving skills.

John just looked at the situation for what seemed to me like a really long time, before offering to help me get out of the ditch. "Are you upset with me?" I asked.

"No," came his response. Then he added, "It can happen to anyone. I've backed into ditches before, too."

Relief washed all down me as I remembered that his gentleness was one of the traits that had attracted me to him in the first place.

The lighthearted nuggets at the beginning of this devotion are just part of what the book of Hebrews is all about. It has so much more to teach, and gentleness is one of those many other teachings that can be learned from a study of Hebrews.

Prayer: Heavenly Father, Your Word is so rich. It has so much to teach us about You and about how to live. Thank You for showing us these things. In Jesus name, Amen.

Thought for the Day: Gentleness is a wonderful trait to cultivate in our lives. The next time you are confronted with a situation where you could respond harshly, work on responding gently instead.

Day Two: Pass Me Not, O Gentle Savior

By Shirley

Worship Hymn Focus
Pass Me Not, O Gentle Savior
1868 by Frances (Fanny) J. Crosby

God's gentleness helps us gain a fuller understanding of how to cultivate and exhibit the fruit of gentleness in our own lives.

Jesus said "Come to me, all you who are weary and burdened, and I will give you rest. Take my yoke upon you and learn from me; for I am gentle and humble in heart, and you will find rest for your souls" (Matthew 11:28-29).

I am reminded of the gentleness of Jesus when I think of the account of blind Bartimaeus in Mark 10:46-52. He heard that Jesus was coming by and cried out for Jesus to have mercy on him. Mark tells us that Jesus stopped and commanded they bring this man to Him. Jesus gently asked Bartimaeus what he wanted. When Bartimaeus said he wanted to receive his sight, Jesus healed him, telling him that his faith made him whole.

As Jesus dealt with people, He was gentle and tender. Through Scripture we learn that God is almighty and to be feared. Fearing God means that we have reverence, awe, and respect for God and His authority and power. These and other characteristics of God highlight His gentleness. We learn how

He deals with us and gain hope for when we go through difficult experiences. We rest on "the eternal God" who "is [our] refuge, and underneath *are* the everlasting arms; and he shall thrust out the enemy from before [us] and shall say, 'Destroy *them*'" (Deuteronomy 33:27).

Frances (Fanny) J. Crosby, who wrote the captivating hymn "Pass Me Not, O Gentle Savior," had a bit in common with Bartimaeus. She was also blind, and this song is a prayer that asks our gentle Savior, Jesus, not to pass over us, but to be our advocate (1 John 2:2).

Stanza 1
Pass me not, O gentle Savior,
Hear my humble cry;
While on others Thou art calling,
Do not pass me by.

We begin by recognizing that Jesus is "the Christ, the Son of the living God" (Matthew 16:16). We recognize that He is also the "mediator between God and men" (1 Timothy 2:5). Since "the eyes of the Lord are on the righteous and his ears are open to their prayer" (1 Peter 3:12), we ask Him to hear our cry, or prayer, while acknowledging that He is able to help us.

Refrain
Savior, Savior,
Hear my humble cry,
While on others Thou art calling,

Do not pass me by.

The refrain reminds us of Psalm 51:1, "Have mercy on me, O God, according to your steadfast love; according to your abundant mercy blot out my transgressions." Since we are cognizant of our sin, we ask the Lord not to pass over us because of the hardness of our hearts, but to hear our cries for help and save us.

Stanza 2
Let me at Thy throne of mercy
Find a sweet relief;
Kneeling there in deep contrition,
Help my unbelief.

Through our High Priest, we can "draw near to the throne of grace, that we may receive mercy and find grace to help in time of need" (Hebrews 4:14-16). We kneel before His throne in "repentance that leads to salvation" (2 Corinthians 7:10). We must come to our High Priest in the same way that the father brought his son to Jesus for healing. We must say "I believe; help my unbelief" (Mark 9:24)!

Stanza 3
Trusting only in Thy merit,
Would I seek Thy face;
Heal my wounded, broken spirit,
Save me by Thy grace.

There is nothing we can do to earn our salvation, thus we must trust in Christ's merit, in His shed blood that atoned for our sin. We seek His face (Psalm 27:8) and healing for our spirit (Ephesians 2:12) as we ask Him to save us by His grace (Ephesians 2:8-9). God's gentleness is seen in His grace and other characteristics.

Stanza 4
Thou the spring of all my comfort,
More than life to me,
Whom have I on earth beside Thee,
Whom in Heav'n but Thee.

Jesus was gentle in His exchange with the Samaritan woman, when He said "…whoever drinks the water I give them will never thirst. Indeed, the water I give them will become in them a spring of water welling up to eternal life" (John 4:14). We express that our relationship with Jesus is our highest priority, we recognize that no one on earth or heaven can save us, and that "it is good to be near God" who is our refuge (Psalm 73:28).

Prayer: Heavenly Father, thank You for Your gentleness as You draw us to Yourself. Enable us to depend upon You for our help and salvation. In Jesus' name, Amen.

Thought for the Day: Our gentle Savior extends His mercy and grace to us.

Day Three: Be Gentle with Others, Even Strangers
By Harriet

Today's Bible Nugget

On what things do angels long to look according to 1 Peter 1:12? The previous verses in 1 Peter 1 give the answer. Suffering and glory and faith tested by fire—these are the beauties on which angels long to look. And these marvels are woven through the stories of human suffering. What makes this so beautiful and so marvelous as to attract the eyes of angels? These stories of human suffering mixed with faith, hope, and eternal glory reflect the sufferings of Christ and the glory that followed (1 Peter 1:7, 11).

As soon as the man walked into the room, with one look I knew his problem was more than I could treat. I sent him directly to see one of the doctors at the doctors' station we had set up. His skin was pulled taut across his arms like someone who had been badly burned, but it was smooth, without the variations in texture usually caused by burn scars. His facial features were distorted by the pull of his skin. But a look at his arms, hands, and feet showed the same taut, pulled skin. And the man told me his skin hurt. That was his chief complaint that day. I nodded and led him to an available doctor.

I was working as a nurse in a medical clinic in Honduras on a high school mission trip I had agreed to chaperone. It was a two-week trip and one of the weeks only required me to chaperone the students on the trip, but the other week called for me to polish off my somewhat rusty nursing skills and use them in a medical clinic. Fortunately, our doctor recognized the man's condition and was able to give him a prescription for a soothing ointment and also make a referral to the hospital in Tegucigalpa, the capital of Honduras, for the man and his sister whom he told us had the same skin problem. Then the man went to our foot washing station.

Every patient who came through our clinic saw either a doctor or nurse, got vitamins, eyeglasses, or meds if they needed them, stopped in a room where they heard the gospel, and then went to the last station where our students put their feet in a pan of warm soapy water and washed them. The patients all loved the foot washing station. Most, if not all, had walked to our remote clinic barefoot or in sandals and some from long distances. But this man had a reaction I will never forget. He cried.

Tears streamed down the taut, painful skin on his distorted face as the students gently touched his feet with soapy water, a clean washcloth, and their hands. An adult on the trip quickly rushed over to him worried that the process might be hurting him. But he was not in pain. Through his tears he began to explain that he had suffered all his life not just his painful (inherited, as it turned out) skin disorder, but also shame. He said people didn't like to look at him, much less touch him, but these students were touching his feet and gently washing them. He told us it was the first human touch he'd received in a very long time.

The students extending kindness and gentleness to this man was evidence of who they were. Their fruit was on display as evidence that they were Christ-followers as they offered gentleness freely and abundantly to this lonely, isolated man.

Be gentle with others. In the case of this man whom I encountered at the medical clinic in Honduras, I could tell as soon as I saw him that he was suffering. As it turned out, he had suffered from this affliction all of his life. There was help available, though, if he followed up on his appointment at the hospital, which I later learned he did and was helped along with his sister. But the point is this—I knew he was suffering the minute I saw him. That is not the case with everyone we encounter in life. Many suffer silently from an affliction, loss, or trial they choose to keep private. As Christians when we suffer, we are reminded that our Savior suffered, too. We are reflecting the sufferings of Jesus, and we will someday get to partake of the glory that follows.

Prayer: Heavenly Father, open our eyes to the suffering around us and even when we don't see another person's pain, keep us mindful that it doesn't mean they are not in pain. Increase our gentleness with others. In Jesus' name,

Amen.

Thought for the Day: Let the fruit of gentleness manifest in you as you go through this life. Angels are watching.

Day Four: Speak Gently[14]

By Shirley

Worship Hymn Focus
Speak Gently

1847 by G. W. Hangford

We continue thinking about being gentle with others by digging a little deeper into what it means to exhibit the fruit of gentleness. Being gentle in our actions with others requires us to be totally dependent upon God as we choose to treat each person with tenderness and calmness.

We all struggle at times being gentle with others. One of the areas in which we often have difficulty being gentle is with our words.

The Bible has a lot to say about our words. Proverbs 15:4 says, "a gentle tongue is a tree of life…" (ESV). We see examples of those who spoke gently and pacified or calmed people and situations. And, of course, we have examples of those who spoke harshly and aggravated people and situations.

The thought-provoking hymn, "Speak Gently," written by G. W. Hangford, reminds us of the benefits and results of speaking gently and helps explain how "gracious words are like a honeycomb, sweetness to the soul and health to the

---

[14] Speak Gently (hymntime.com)

body" (Proverbs 16:24).

Stanza 1
Speak gently; it is better far
To rule by love than fear;
Speak gently: let no harsh word mar
The good we may do here.

We are to rule and be ruled by love, not fear, as we learn from 1 John 4:18, "There is no fear in love. But perfect love drives out fear." When we speak gently out of love, we are able to do more good than when we speak harshly and mar any good that could have come from that exchange.

Stanza 2
Speak gently! Love doth whisper low
The vows that true hearts bind;
And gently friendship's accents flow;
Affection's voice is kind.

When we speak gently to those whom we love, our friendships grow and our affections blossom. Let us "put on love, which binds [us] all together in perfect harmony" (Colossians 3:14).

Stanza 3
Speak gently to the little child;
Its love be sure to gain.
Teach it in accents soft and mild;
It may not long remain.

Speak gently to children when teaching them about God and His commands using soft and mild vocal tones (Deuteronomy 6:7).

Stanza 4
Speak gently to the young, for they
Will have enough to bear;
Pass through this world as best they may,
'Tis full of anxious care.

We are to "tell the next generation the praiseworthy deeds of the LORD, his power, and the wonders he has done" (Psalm 78:4) so that while they walk through their lives, they will be prepared for and know how to honor God as they respond to all the things they will face.

Stanza 5
Speak gently to the agèd one,
Grieve not the care-worn heart;
The sands of life are nearly run;
Let such in peace depart.

Speak gently with patience to the elderly, encouraging and exhorting them to continue living lives that honor God (1 Timothy 5:1-3). We are to respect and honor them in their twilight years and not let our attitudes, words, or actions cause them grief, sadness, or pain.

Stanza 6
Speak gently, kindly to the poor;
Let no harsh tone be heard;
They have enough they must endure,
Without an unkind word.

Likewise, speak gently to the poor because they often hear only unkind or harsh words. We are also to "speak up for those who cannot speak for themselves" (Proverbs 31:8-9) because they are enduring many hardships.

Stanza 7
Speak gently to the erring; know
They must have toiled in vain;
Perchance unkindness made them so;
Oh! win them back again.

When we see a Christ-follower sinning, we are not to speak harshly or accuse them, instead we are to "restore that person gently" (Galatians 6:1). When we see non-Christ-followers living in sin, we are to teach them gently "in the hope that God will grant them repentance leading them to a knowledge of the truth, and that they will come to their senses and escape from the trap of the devil, who has taken them captive to do his will" (2 Timothy 2:25-26).

Stanza 8
Speak gently: He who gave His life
To bend man's stubborn will,
When elements were fierce in strife,

Said to them, Peace, be still!

Our example for speaking gently is Jesus Christ, who came to earth to live as fully God and fully man taking upon Himself our sin and the punishment we deserved for that sin. During all the storms in our lives, He still speaks gently, calming our fears and anxieties.

Stanza 9
Speak gently: 'tis a little thing
Dropped in the heart's deep well;
The good, the joy which it may bring,
Eternity shall tell.

When we speak gently, we do not know the immediate, long-term, or eternal effect our words may have on others. We are to "Let [our] conversation be always full of grace, seasoned with salt, so that [we] may know how to answer everyone" (Colossians 4:6).

Prayer: Heavenly Father, thank You for the gentle way You have dealt with us and for Your Word which teaches us how we can exhibit the fruit of gentleness in all we think, say, and do. In Jesus' name, Amen.

Thought for the Day: God is near, teaching, and enabling us to speak gently (Philippians 4:5).

Day Five: Be Gentle with Yourself

By Harriet

Today's Bible Nugget

How do you feel today? Perhaps you are tired because you didn't get enough sleep last night. Or maybe you are frustrated by the economy or world events. Maybe your career is not moving as fast as you would like it to. Or did you wake up today thinking, "I feel like a king! I feel like a Priest, like a chosen person!" Well, that's what you are according to 1 Peter 2:9 which says, "But you are a chosen race, a royal priesthood, a holy nation, a people for God's own possession, that you may proclaim the excellencies of Him who has called you out of darkness into His marvelous light."

"Be gentle with yourself" is an expression we sometimes hear. It's good counsel. Life is full of ups and downs, and we navigate both better if we treat ourselves with gentleness whether we are up or down. But what does being gentle with ourselves look like, especially as one of the manifestations of this fruit of the spirit? And why would someone need to be gentle with oneself if things are going great in one's life?

I remember learning about distress and eustress in one of my college nursing classes. These are defined as stress coming from totally opposite sources. Distress is stress a person experiences when difficult, negative things happen;

whereas eustress is stress that a person experiences from positive occurrences in their lives. Eustress is generally seen in a positive light as stress that motivates someone to overcome an obstacle or achieve greater success. Still, I learned that both affect the body in similar ways. They can raise a person's blood pressure or keep them from getting enough sleep, whether they are tossing and turning all night because of some terrible misfortune or tossing and turning because they have a great new contract at work with a deadline hanging over their head. Take having a baby for instance, or more specifically the desire to have a child. Constant failure to achieve this goal and get pregnant, or repeated miscarriages have physical effects on the body that can keep it from functioning optimally. The same is true for achieving the desired goal of becoming pregnant. The body still goes through a lot with a pregnancy and for those who end up adopting, they too find themselves facing many stresses.

Good things and bad things effect a person and call for gentleness.

If you put the phrase "be gentle with yourself" in a search bar, a lot of self-help sites pop up. I clicked on one and found it full of good suggestions, but they were all self-oriented types of things a person could do to accept themselves, especially in times of distress. They were not unhelpful, and I am not criticizing taking practical steps to apply this concept. In fact, I'll pass on one I heard from my late widowed mother-in-law. Once when I was going under some stress with a child in a hospital, she told me, "After my husband was killed unexpectedly in that plane crash, I learned that if I found myself feeling particularly down, I'd let myself do whatever I wanted to do as long as it was not illegal or unethical. If I wanted to go shopping, I went shopping. If I wanted to eat chocolate candy, I ate chocolate candy. If I wanted to soak in a hot tub for an hour, I did it."

But what are all these self-help tips missing? They are not looking above. Gentleness is a gift from God as one of the fruit of the Spirit. A fruit is how we tell what the tree is. We know by its fruit if it's an apple tree or a pear tree, and so forth. Likewise, the fruit of the Spirit show what type of people we are. Specifically, they show we are Christ-followers filled with His spirit. And studying God's Word as Spirit-filled Christ-followers will help us see ourselves the way God sees us. He loved us enough to send Jesus to die for us. We are in fact, "a chosen race, a royal priesthood, a holy nation, a people for God's own possession," so we can and should manifest gentleness and other fruit of the Spirit, even with ourselves.

Prayer: Heavenly Father, fill us with Your spirit so we will bear Your fruit. Help us to be gentle with others and also with ourselves. In Jesus' name, Amen.

Thought for the Day: When you deal with yourself, you are dealing with God's treasure. Be gentle with His treasure.

Week Ten:

Faithfulness

Nuggets of Wonder from the New Testament book of Prophecy

As with the Old Testament, there is prophecy in the New Testament, primarily in the book of Revelation. There are a few other spots in the New Testament that contain some prophecy, such as in the book of Matthew, but Revelation is the only book that is entirely prophecy, and it also does not fit into any other category. (Matthew fits in the gospels, for instance.)

Revelation is by far one of the most challenging books in the Bible to understand. Its prophecy is about the events that will occur in the last days. The name comes from the Greek term *apokalypsis*, meaning "unveiling" or "revelation." The book tells of the invisible forces and spiritual powers at work in the world and in the heavenly realms, including forces at war against the church. Although unseen, these powers control future events and realities.[15]

Written by the apostle John when he was exiled on the Island of Patmos near the end of his life, the only book in this New Testament Prophecy category is Revelation.

---

[15] The Book of Revelation, a Prophecy of Warning and Hope (learnreligions.com) accessed 8/3/22

Fruit of the Spirit, Faithfulness

This week the focus is on the fruit of the Spirit, faithfulness. The Greek word is *pistis*, which means we are dependable and trustworthy because we are confident in God and His faithfulness. Faithfulness is proof of the Holy Spirit's presence and work in our lives.

"With this in mind, we constantly pray for you, that our God may make you worthy of his calling, and that by his power he may bring to fruition your every desire for goodness and your every deed prompted by faith" (2 Thessalonians 1:11).

Day One: Would Others Know Who You Are by Clues?

By Harriet

Today's Bible Nugget

Can you keep a secret? Apparently, Jesus can. Revelation 19:12 says that Jesus has a name which only He knows. The person in this verse is the rider on the white horse. How do we know this person is Jesus? The verses before and after give us hints. Verse eleven says this person is called "Faithful and True" and He judges in righteousness. And verse thirteen says He is clothed in a robe dipped in blood and His name is called The Word of God. But it is verse twelve that intrigues me. It says, "And His eyes are a flame of fire, and upon His head are many diadems; and He has a name written upon Him which no one knows except Himself" (NASB).

I have always found this a fascinating verse. What is Jesus' secret name? Why wouldn't He tell anyone what it is? Interestingly, if we dig further, it turns out that another passage in Revelation says that someday we will have a name known only to us, too. We find that odd fact in Revelation 2:17 which says, "Whoever has ears, let them hear what the Spirit says to the churches. To the one who is victorious, I will give some of the hidden manna. I will also give that person a white stone with a new name written on it, known only to the one who receives it. Whoever has ears, let them hear what the Spirit says to the churches."

Is heaven just going to be a place full of secrets? I don't think so. First, I'll admit that Revelation is the hardest book in the entire Bible to understand. There might even be debate as to who the overcomers in this verse are. Are they every believer who has overcome sin by accepting Christ as their Savior and having their sin covered by His blood? Or are the overcomers a specific group of believers? I cannot answer those questions with absolute certainty, and neither can I explain with confidence what the secret names are. The best explanation I have ever read came from a book entitled, "The Global Destiny People" written by a Nigerian writer friend of mine named David Olawoyin. In his book, David offered an explanation for these secret names that I hadn't heard in the two-year inductive study of Revelation I attended some years ago, or anywhere else. David suggests in his book that the reason these names are known only to the bearer is that they are who that person really is, the special person God created us to be, which is unique and different from anyone else. Thus, the name is only known to us not because it is a secret, and others don't know our names but because we alone are the unique person God created us to be and no one else can fill that spot. That unique spot in God's eternal plan is known only to us. It's who we alone are. No one else knows how to be us but us.

Though speculating on what this unusual Bible nugget

may be all about is interesting, there is a more practical point in this nugget. I said in the nugget that the person described in Revelation 19:12 is Jesus. How do I know that? The verse does not give the name Jesus. I know because of the clues given about the person described in the verse. He is the rider on the white horse, clothed in a robe dipped in blood, and His name is "The Word of God."

A quick cross-reference to John 1:1 and we find this, "In the beginning was the Word, and the Word was with God, and the Word was God." A little further down in John 1:14, we read, "The Word became flesh and made his dwelling among us." So, who do we know from Scripture was with God in the beginning and was God but then became flesh and dwelt among people? The answer, of course, is Jesus. (Don't you just love detective work?) There is another clue in the Revelation passage in today's nugget too—He is the one called "Faithful and True."

If someone only had clues about you or me, would they be able to figure out who we are? Would they be able to figure out whose we are—that we are followers of Christ? We have been looking at the fruit of the Spirit in this devotional book. One of this fruit is faithfulness. A faithful person is true to his or her word. If they say they will do something, they do it. They are someone others can count on. When others look at our actions do they see us exhibiting faithfulness? How about any of the other fruit of the Spirit we have looked at in this book?

Prayer: Father, may we manifest the fruit of the Spirit in our lives. May we reflect that we are Your children in our lives in such a way that people who meet us can tell by the manner in which we conduct ourselves that we belong to You. In Jesus' name, Amen.

Thought for the Day: If someone only had clues about you, would they be able to figure out who you are?

Day Two: Great is Thy Faithfulness

By Shirley

Worship Hymn Focus
Great is Thy Faithfulness
1923 by Thomas O. Chisholm

Through our understanding of the faithfulness of God, we gain a fuller understanding of how to cultivate and exhibit the fruit of faithfulness in our own lives.

Reading the Bible, from Genesis through Revelation, we see God's faithfulness as we trace the work of His hand in and through everything. We can also look back at our lives and see His faithfulness that has empowered us to walk through all kinds of circumstances while we have learned to trust Him more and more.

We see God's faithfulness demonstrated through His unchanging nature. In Malachi 3:6 God said, "I the Lord do not change." This means that His character is not only consistent, but it also means that the rules He set forth for us to follow do not change. Our understanding of self-control which comes from our understanding of God's character, enables us to gain a better understanding of how to cultivate and exhibit the fruit of self-control in our lives.

In our walk as Christ-followers, we manifest the fruit of the Spirit, faithfulness, in response to God's faithfulness. The exuberant hymn, "Great is Thy Faithfulness," written by

Thomas O. Chisholm describes the magnificent faithfulness of God and reminds us of various reasons we can trust Him to be faithful. The inspiration for this hymn is Lamentations 3:21-23.

"Yet this I call to mind and therefore I have hope: Because of the Lord's great love we are not consumed, for his compassions never fail. They are new every morning; great is your faithfulness."

Stanza 1
Great is Thy faithfulness, O God my Father;
There is no shadow of turning with Thee;
Thou changest not, Thy compassions, they fail not;
As Thou hast been Thou forever wilt be.

What a glorious truth—God never changes. As we sing, we are reminded that "every good and perfect gift is from above, coming down from the Father of the heavenly lights, who does not change like shifting shadows" (James 1:17). We also know that He will keep His promises to us and that He is "the Alpha and the Omega… who is, and who was, and who is to come" (Revelation 1:8).

Refrain
Great is Thy faithfulness! Great is Thy faithfulness!
Morning by morning new mercies I see:
All I have needed Thy hand hath provided—
Great is Thy faithfulness, Lord, unto me!

As Christ-followers, we can look back to moments in our lives when things were very difficult and remember that faithful God was there to strengthen, enable, and comfort us. We see God's faithfulness in that "His divine power has given us everything we need for a godly life through our knowledge of him who called us by his own glory and goodness" (2 Peter 1:3). These are amazing reasons to praise Him!

Stanza 2
Summer and winter and springtime and harvest,
Sun, moon, and stars in their courses above
Join with all nature in manifold witness
To Thy great faithfulness, mercy, and love.

What a beautiful expression echoing what David wrote in Psalm 19:1-4, "The heavens declare the glory of God; the skies proclaim the work of his hands. Day after day they pour forth speech; night after night they reveal knowledge. They have no speech, they use no words; no sound is heard from them. Yet their voice goes out into all the earth, their words to the ends of the world." The seasons and the celestial bodies, engaging their many different parts, join everything in creation to praise God for His faithfulness, mercy, and love.

Stanza 3
Pardon for sin and a peace that endureth,
Thine own dear presence to cheer and to guide,
Strength for today and bright hope for tomorrow—

Blessings all mine, with ten thousand beside!

We praise "the God and Father of our Lord Jesus Christ! In his great mercy he has given us new birth into a living hope through the resurrection of Jesus Christ from the dead, and into an inheritance that can never perish, spoil or fade. This inheritance is kept in heaven for you, who through faith are shielded by God's power until the coming of the salvation that is ready to be revealed in the last time" (1 Peter 1:3-5). The result of this pardon, new birth, and inheritance, is the enduring peace that comes from His presence guiding and encouraging us in our walk with Him. Another part of the spiritual blessings He gives us is that we will have the strength that we need to walk confidently through whatever we encounter during our day. His indwelling Holy Spirit also gives us bright hope for our future.

Prayer: Heavenly Father, thank You for Your enduring, unchangeable, and everlasting faithfulness. While we grow closer in our relationship with You, enable our confidence and trust in You to grow as we exhibit the fruit of faithfulness. In Jesus' name, Amen.

Thought for the Day: God's presence cheers, guides, and gives us strength for today and bright hope for tomorrow.

Day Three: Longing for Home

By Harriet

Today's Bible Nugget

The book of Revelation speaks about people who "dwell on the earth" in the end times, "earth dwellers" or "EDs" for short as we called them in an inductive Bible study on Revelation I once attended. These EDs will face testing according to Revelation 3:10, they will worship the beast (Revelation 13:8, 12, & 17:8), and be drunk with immorality (17:2).

This sounds just awful, doesn't it? If we happened to still be here when the end comes, would we be EDs? The earth is where we live so in that sense, we are earth dwellers. It's helpful to look at the Greek to get better insight into what an ED is. The Greek word is *ghay katoikeo*. *Ghay* simply means earth. But *katoikeo* helps explain what EDs really are. This word means to house permanently and denotes intensity. In other words, EDs are people who are attached to the earth as if it were their permanent home. The contrast to this can be found in Hebrews 11:13 and 16 where we read of a people who are strangers and exiles on the earth; people who long for a better country, a heavenly one. Drawing that distinction, it is a relief to see that Christ-followers are the ones looking for a heavenly home and not attached to the earth, believing it to be their permanent home. Whew!

Understanding the Greek words used in this passage is helpful. It's reassuring to think that if we put ourselves in this end-time scenario, we would not be the "earth-dwellers" who face testing, worship the beast, and act so immorally as to be said we are drunk on immorality. But the passage in the eleventh chapter of Hebrews does not paint a rosy picture either. Over and over, it tells of people who act with faithfulness through all sorts of trials and tribulations. They hold on in faith, yes, but their lives are still filled with trials, difficulties, and challenges of all kinds. Some are even dire, yet they stay faithful.

Faithfulness can be defined as staying true to something or someone. In an earlier devotion it was explained as being a person who is true—someone who can be counted on. This quality occurs because that person is dedicated to and loyal to something or someone. God is faithful. He is steadfast. He never changes and can be counted on. We are to be faithful too, as these heroes of the faith in Hebrews 11 were.

Hebrews 11 is one of my favorite passages in all of Scripture. I love that it names heroes of the faith. I love that when I look at my less than perfect life, I can see from this passage that heroes of the faith had imperfect and even downright difficult lives, too. I love that these faith heroes didn't give up, but still searched for a better land, a heavenly one. In other words, they were not "*ghay katoikeos*." They were not EDs tightly attached to this earth. They knew this earth was not their home. They knew they were just passing through enroute to a better place. This thought has given me hope many times in my life.

As I have mentioned many times before, I was born and raised in a foreign land. I loved the lush, beautiful, tropical land of my childhood and when my family left and came back to America, I was heartbroken. Ever since then I have felt a personal sense of internal confusion when asked where home is. To this day I will answer that question with two answers. In my heart, my hometowns are Bluefield, West Virginia, where I lived during my middle and high school years and where my parents then continued to live for many more years after that, and Ogbomoso, Nigeria, where I spent my childhood years. I am in some ways a person without a country. This feeling, as it turns out, is common among people like me who have citizenship in one country but were born and raised in another. I get it. I understand the feeling of longing for a home that is somewhere other than where my body presently resides. I've wrestled with that feeling most of my life, especially the first few years back in America as an early teenager. That is another reason I love this passage so much.

But the top reason I love this passage in Hebrews 11 is found in verse 16, "Instead, they were longing for a better country—a heavenly one. Therefore God is not ashamed to be called their God, for he has prepared a city for them." This verse sums up faithfulness: the people demonstrate their faithfulness to God by continuing to long for heaven rather than becoming content with their earthly homes and God demonstrates His faithfulness and tender love for His people by preparing for them the homes they long for, and He is proud of them and not ashamed for unbelievers to know that He is their God.

Prayer: Heavenly Father, this earth is not our home. We are reminded of that daily in so many ways. Walk with us as we face the challenges we must face. Keep us faithful to You. In Jesus' name, Amen.

Thought for the Day: Are you becoming attached to this world as if it's your permanent home? Or are you longing for a better home—a heavenly one? Are you the kind of person of whom God is not ashamed to be called your God?

Day Four: Standing on the Promises

By Shirley

Worship Hymn Focus
Standing on the Promises
1886 by Russell K. Carter

We began this devotional book talking about God's holiness, the fertile soil in which the fruit of the Spirit flourishes. We looked at the R. C. Sproul quote that the holiness of God "…is basic to our whole understanding of God and of Christianity."[16]

Through the Holy Spirit-inspired Bible we are able to know who God is and learn that His "faithfulness continues through all generations… and it endures" (Psalm 119:90). In this devotional book we have gone to the Bible for insight into the nuggets and fruit of the Spirit. In the same way, as Christ-followers we stand on the promises of God in His Word. It is through the Holy Spirit-inspired Word that we are able to know who God is and learn about His faithfulness throughout all generations.

The words of God in the Bible are as enduring and unchangeable as His character. "Heaven and earth will pass

---

[16] Sproul, R. C. (2009). *The Holiness of God*. Tyndale House Publishers.
https://www.amazon.com/KindleEditions/B00ZRPX97C, page 12, location 326.

away, but [God's] words will never pass away" (Matthew 24:35). The pages of the Bible are filled with eternal truth because Scripture came by "prophets," who "spoke from God as they were carried along by the Holy Spirit" (2 Peter 1:21). God's Word is truth (John 17:17). It is "the light of the gospel that displays the glory of Christ, who is the image of God" (2 Corinthians 4:4). God's Word is "a lamp for my feet, a light on my path" (Psalm 119:105) to guide us.

In God's Word, He "has given us everything we need for a godly life through our knowledge of him who called us by his own glory and goodness. Through these he has given us his very great and precious promises, so that through them you may participate in the divine nature, having escaped the corruption in the world caused by evil desires" (2 Peter 1:3-4).

How are we to respond to these great and precious promises of God? Russell K. Carter helps us express our response in the triumphant hymn, "Standing on the Promises."

Stanza 1
Standing on the promises of Christ my King,
Through eternal ages let His praises ring,
Glory in the highest, I will shout and sing,
Standing on the promises of God.

As Christ-followers we are dependent upon the promises of God. We are able to stand, or depend upon, the promises of God because they are made by Jesus Christ, the King—our King. Since His Word and His promises are true we sing and shout our praises to Him. We know that "no matter how many promises God has made, they are 'Yes' in Christ. And so through him the 'Amen' is spoken by us to the glory of God" (2 Corinthians 1:20). In Jesus Christ we have the assurance that God's promises are true.

Refrain
Standing, standing,
Standing on the promises of God my Savior;
Standing, standing,
I'm standing on the promises of God.

Because of the promises of God our Savior, "We have this as a sure and steadfast anchor of the soul" (Hebrews 6:19). When standing on God's promises in Christ, we can walk through our lives secure in our relationship with God and His faithfulness to us.

Stanza 2
Standing on the promises that cannot fail,
When the howling storms of doubt and fear assail,
By the living Word of God I shall prevail,
Standing on the promises of God.

God's promises cannot fail for "it is impossible for God to lie" (Hebrews 6:18). So even "though now for a little while you may have had to suffer grief in all kinds of trials" (1 Peter

1:6) we shall prevail by trusting in and firmly standing upon the Word of God.

Stanza 3
Standing on the promises I now can see
Perfect, present cleansing in the blood for me;
Standing in the liberty where Christ makes free,
Standing on the promises of God.

After coming to a saving knowledge of Christ, we better understand the perfect, present cleansing we have through "the blood of Jesus" that "purifies us from all sin" (1 John 1:7). Because of the shed blood of Jesus, "Christ has set us free" so we are to "stand firm... and not let [ourselves] be burdened again by a yoke of slavery" (Galatians 5:1) to sin.

Stanza 4
Standing on the promises of Christ the Lord,
Bound to Him eternally by love's strong cord,
Overcoming daily with the Spirit's sword,
Standing on the promises of God.

We stand on the promises of Christ the Lord to save us. We are eternally bound or tethered to God because He sent Jesus into the world to atone for our sins so that through Him we can live victoriously over sin (1 John 4:9-10). We can withstand and overcome whatever comes our way by fighting with the "sword of the Spirit, which is the word of God" (Ephesians 6:17).

Stanza 5
Standing on the promises I cannot fall,
List'ning every moment to the Spirit's call,
Resting in my Savior as my all in all,
Standing on the promises of God.

As we stand on the promises of God, we are strengthened to obey His Word. He is "able to keep [us] from stumbling and to present [us] before his glorious presence without fault and with great joy" (Jude 1:24). When we are sensitive to the Holy Spirit's prompting to live according to God's commands and to know Him, we can rest in our Savior—Christ our all in all (Colossians 3:11).

Prayer: Heavenly Father, thank You for Your Word, through which we learn about You and know what You require of us. Thank You that because You are faithful and Your Word is true, we can stand firmly on Your promises. In Jesus' name, Amen.

Thought for the Day: By the living Word of God we shall prevail. – Russell K. Carter

Day Five: Never Changing

By Harriet

Today's Bible Nugget

"There is no book that has less quotes of the Old Testament than the book of Revelation, but there is no book that uses the Old Testament more than the book of Revelation." This is another quote by Dr. Peter Gentry, Septuagint scholar and my Sunday school teacher for many years. Dr. Gentry explained that rather than quoting the Old Testament directly, Revelation alludes to it. For instance, in Revelation 1:12-14 the Old Testament is alluded to at least four times; golden lampstands can be found in Exodus 25:37, 37:23, and Zechariah 4:2; the term "son of man" in Ezekiel 1:26 and Daniel 7:13 (often translated only as "man" since Son of Man is a term that simply means human), a robe with a golden girdle in Daniel 10:5, and hair that is white like wool in Daniel 7:9. And that is only two verses from the book of Revelation. To cite all the examples would make this devotion way too long.

It is not surprising that the last book of the New Testament contains so many references from books in the Old Testament, thus demonstrating the consistency that runs throughout Scripture. God is the same God today that He was in Old Testament days, and He will remain the same throughout all eternity. Malachi 3:6 states it plainly when it says, "I the LORD do not change." Hebrews 13:8 says it about Jesus, too, "Jesus Christ is the same yesterday and today and forever."

How many changes do we experience in our lifetimes as we go from childhood to old age? In a previous devotion, I mentioned the two places I consider my hometowns. I cannot return to my childhood home in Nigeria very easily, but from what some childhood friends who have been back in recent years tell me, much has changed. One of the things I treasure about my high school hometown in West Virginia is that though there have been some changes since I moved away to attend college and then married and settled elsewhere, much is still the same. I was a cheerleader in high school who had the exhilarating experience of cheering for a state championship football team. When the air turns crisp in the fall, my high school still plays competitive football in that same stadium. The coach for the past several decades is a high school friend and he still leads his team to state championships from time to time. It's so nice to be able to travel back in the fall, renew old friendships, and watch great high school football played in that same stadium.

Sometimes life changes slowly, but sometimes it changes so quickly we are knocked flat by the change and find ourselves struggling to adjust to our new situation. Our nation's laws even change. When I first learned to drive the top speed limit on a highway was fifty-five miles an hour. If

I drove my car at seventy miles an hour, I could get a speeding ticket. Today I can sail along at seventy and never worry about getting a ticket. In this case the speed limit law change was welcomed by me, but there are many other cases where changes in my life have not been so welcome.

In this ever-changing world, it is comforting to know that the God we worship always remains the same. His truths that we find through reading and studying His Word remain the same, too. This is stated plainly in Isaiah 40:8 where find these words, "The grass withers and the flowers fall, but the word of our God endures forever."

The wonderful fruit of the Spirit that God's Word tells us about in the fifth chapter of Galatians and that we have meditated upon in so many ways in this devotional book have never changed and will never change. No matter how harsh the world around us may become, God still sits on His throne, He remains faithful and true, His love is eternal, and the fruit He gives to His children is and will always be love, joy, peace, patience, kindness, goodness, faithfulness, gentleness, and self-control.

Prayer: Heavenly Father, as this book winds up, we pause to think back on all the ways You teach us through Your life-giving words that we find in Scripture. Thank You for giving us Your Word. Open our eyes to understand it better. In Jesus' name, Amen.

Thought for the Day: God's Word as read in the Bible is a treasure, whether learned in small nuggets at a time or whole book or topical studies. In this book we've combined two—small nuggets and a topical study on the fruit of the Spirit. Keep it up. Keep studying. Keep digging for nuggets.

About the Authors

Harriet E. Michael

Born in the jungles of Nigeria, West Africa, in the heart of the Niger River Delta, as the daughter of missionaries, Harriet spent her childhood in Nigeria. Her carefree tropical childhood ended when a civil war broke out and her family returned to America. They settled in the beautiful mountains of Bluefield, West Virginia, where Harriet attended junior high and high school.

She is a child of two countries. To this day, both places live in her heart and come out in her writings. Since her first published article in 2010, she is now an award-winning freelance writer and author with ten books she has either authored or co-authored, and several hundred published articles, short stories, and devotions. One of her books won the prestigious Selah Award in 2021, taking first place in nonfiction books. Her writings have also won a second place Selah and a first place Cascade Award.

Harriet's writings are as diverse as her life has been. Though she writes primarily nonfiction pieces, she has penned one novel and has some children's stories in her head that she hopes to someday have in print.

Harriet holds a BS in nursing from West Virginia University but has discovered her passion for writing. She and John, her husband of over forty years, now live in Kentucky. They have four grown children and five grandchildren. When she's not writing she enjoys substitute teaching at a Christian school, gardening, and cooking.

Follow her on:
Website: www.harrietemichael.com
Facebook:
https//www.facebook.com/harrietmichaelauthor
Blog: www.harrietemichael.blogspot.com
Amazon: amazon.com/author/harrietemichael

Shirley Crowder

Shirley Crowder was born in a mission guest house under the shade of a mango tree in Nigeria, West Africa, where her parents served as missionaries. She and co-author Harriet E. Michael grew up together on the mission field and have been lifelong friends. Shirley is passionate about disciple-making, which is manifested in and through a myriad of ministry opportunities: biblical counseling, teaching Bible studies, writing, and music.

She is published as an author, co-author, and contributing author of fourteen books. Several of her articles have appeared in "Paper Pulpit" in the Faith section of *The Gadsden Times*, and in a David C. Cook publication. She has also written for Life Bible Study and Woman's Missionary Union. She is a biblical counselor and serves as Vice President of The Addiction Connection.

Shirley has spiritual children, grandchildren, and even

great-grandchildren serving the Lord in various ministry and secular positions throughout the world.

Follow her on:
Facebook: /shirleycrowderauthor
Twitter: @ShirleyJCrowder
Blog: www.throughthelensofscripture.com
Amazon: /author/shirleycrowder

Thank you
for reading our books!

If you enjoyed this devotional,
please consider returning to its
purchase page and leaving a review!

Look for other books
published by

Entrusted Books
an Imprint of
Write Integrity Press

www.WriteIntegrity.com